WordPress for Beginners 2018

A Visual Step-by-Step Guide to Mastering WordPress

Updated January 25th, 2018

Dr. Andy Williams

http://ezseonews.com

What people are saying about previous versions of this book:

"I work in the education department at one of the top academic institutions in the U.S. and if I could hire Dr. Williams to write all of my online training, I wouldn't hesitate..." **Laurie**

"Wow! From someone who is not a beginner to WordPress." **Albert J**

"Definitely the go-to guide! Since WordPress is a pretty easy format to get started on, I was able to make some progress. Then I found WordPress for Beginners and WOW - my progress took off. Having a visual guide with extensive photos really helps those of us who are visual learners. But the best thing to me is that Williams not only describes what to do and how to do it, he explains why you should do it. I'm not a professional tech person and this book is exactly what I needed. I suspect I will continue to refer to it in the future. Highly recommended." **Amazon Customer**

"Nailed It. I have been trying to install a working blog from time to time for the last four years, and of course, have read various books on the subject. It always got more complicated, with dashboards, PHP, SQL, SEO, or a shared WordPress site. This is the one book that does it flawlessly, and the installation actually works just as shown. The screenshots are accurate and most helpful as you step through each learning segment. Having written several technical how-to manuals myself, I recognize a remarkably well structured and logical sequence of easy to learn, bite-sized topics." **Terry O'Hara**

"If you want to have a website but don't know how, this book by Dr. Andy Williams will take you by the hand and walk you through the process of setting up your own blog correctly. He tells you not only exactly how to do it, but also explains the why you are taking the steps he walks you through. The instructions and visuals are clear and easy for anyone to follow." **J. Tanner**

"I Would Give This Book a 5 Plus. I literally started at page one and built my website from scratch without any prior experience because

of this book. It was very easy to read and was laid out in a very logical, step by step order. I would recommend it without hesitation. I was so impressed with this book that I went and ordered several other of the author's books relating to developing an online presence." *GP*

"Clear, practical, and very helpful, WordPress for Beginners takes the reader step by step through the essentials of organizing your online world. Dr. Williams is a great writer and an excellent teacher. Highly recommended!" **Dr. James A. Holmund**

"Great lessons from a great teacher. Andy Williams really has a knack for organizing information in a clear, concise, and to-the-point manner. It is only a matter of following his excellent advice, and you will have a functioning WordPress site up and running in no time." **Prufrock**

"Why can't all guides be like this?" **B J Burton**

"Exemplary teaching. This book is a model of good teaching. Clear, uncluttered, direct. It takes you through the process with admirable clarity. I bought a printed guide to Word Press for twice the price which left me utterly confused - this book should be used as an example of how to teach. Very highly recommended." **Amazon Customer**

"An excellent book. I logged into my account and just followed the book page by page and in no time at all I had a Website mapped out and running. The book is easy to follow and you very quickly learn how WordPress works and how it can be used for writing Blogs, conventional Websites and even combined ones if you are so inclined. This really is an excellent book to have in your programming library and is of great value in helping to steer through the morass of misinformation about WordPress on the web. I have just ordered the paperback version to have by my side which I anticipate will become well-worn into the future." **Dr. A F Gerrard**

"Quite simply the best advice I've found............ Having spent a number of months getting disheartened and frustrated, I bought this book as a last ditch attempt to get my website going before having to pay someone to do it for me. Setting up a website is not something I'd ever done before so I had no technical knowledge at all. Quite simply, this book is superb. It was just like having the web developer sitting next to me at my desk talking me through every little detail. He 'told me' what to ignore (explaining why as he did so), explained what we were doing and why at every step and the pictures aligned to what was on my screen as I went along. Two days later I had a website and now I am actually changing the theme and altering things with confidence. I simply cannot rate this book highly enough. Thank you, Andy!" **Louise Burridge**

"Brilliant - all you need to know to get up and running." S. J. Oswald

"I had to design a website urgently and one I could manage myself. I'd read that to do this I needed a web design programme that offered CMS, Content Control Management and that WordPress was the best programme for the job. I was a complete beginner with no knowledge at all about website design. Before I came across Dr Andy Williams book I'd bought two others and became overwhelmed by the complexity and the jargon.

If you want to design your own website, you don't need any other book than this. If you work through it carefully and methodically you'll quickly learn all the technicalities involved and have the vocabulary to create a website that is visually arresting, the content, of course, is up to you.

Dr. Williams is a natural-born teacher with that special genius of being able to make a complex process easy and interesting to follow. The large-format book is a pleasure to use. It begins with the assumption that the reader knows nothing about WordPress, website hosting, registering and costs. The easy to follow steps takes you through this process to the point where once your website is up and running, the reader can download WordPress, then get to work! Dr. Williams takes you through every aspect of the WordPress 'dashboard,' (the programme's control panel) a place it is important to know well, and where the web designer will spend a lot of time. Once the reader is familiar with this, the design process starts and Dr. Williams again leads the reader step by step through the website building process.

One of the many outstanding features of the book is the use of screenshots that show the reader what to do and where to do it, it's like using a print out of a video. Another indispensable feature is the "Tasks To Complete" sections found at the end of each major learning phase. The reader is given a list of tasks to work through which consolidates what has been learned and offers a comprehensive revision structure that can be revisited as many times as necessary.

"WordPress for Beginners" is not just an outstanding book about WordPress, it is also a model of how this kind of "teaching at a distance," should be done. Dr. Williams has written several other books using the same teaching techniques, we can only hope the list continues to grow." Dr. Gerald Benedict

DISCLAIMER AND TERMS OF USE AGREEMENT

Contents

Who am I & why should you listen to me?

My name is Andy Williams and I am a teacher. In 2001 I gave up teaching in schools where I had been a Science teacher working with students from 11 to 18 years of age. I needed a new challenge, and most of all I wanted to spend more time with my family.

Since then my work (and my hobby), has been to study the search engines and build websites for profit. It's been a long journey and a lot of people have followed me on that voyage by reading my free newsletter published over at ezSEONews.com. My newsletter has covered a wide range of topics relevant to webmasters - that's people who own and build their own website(s). If you are interested, you can sign up to receive my free newsletter too.

In the early days, websites were hand-built using a code called HyperText Markup Language, or HTML for short. To create good-looking websites, you needed to be something of a geek. Tools like Macromedia Dreamweaver (now owned by Adobe), and Microsoft Front Page (discontinued in 2006), were developed to reduce the coding learning curve associated with building a website in HTML, but these tools were expensive.

Then in May 2003, Matt Mullenweg & Mike Little, released a tool that would change the face of website building forever. They called it WordPress.

I have to admit I was a little reluctant to give up my copy of Dreamweaver, but in 2004 I started to experiment with the WordPress platform. At that time, WordPress was just starting to get interesting with the introduction of "plugins". Don't worry, we'll look at those later in the book, but for now just understand that plugins are an easy and pain-free way of adding great new functionality to your website.

Fast-forward to today and WordPress is now the site-building tool of choice for many professionals and enthusiasts alike. Home businesses run by moms & dads, school kids running blogs about their favorite bands, large corporations, and everyone in between, have all turned to WordPress. It's extremely powerful, flexible, produces very professional looking websites or blogs, is relatively easy to use, and perhaps best of all, it's totally free.

Sure, there is a learning curve, but that is where I come in.

With years of experience teaching technical stuff in an easy to understand manner, I am going to take you by the hand and guide you as you construct your very own professional looking website or blog, even if you know absolutely nothing about how to go about this. The only thing you need to know is how to use a web browser. If you have ever searched Google for something, then you already have the skills necessary to follow this book.

I have made this book a step-by-step, visual guide to creating your website. Just follow along with the exercises and in no time at all, you'll be using WordPress like a pro. You'll build a website you can be proud to show your family and friends. In fact, they will probably start asking YOU to help them build their own website.

Excited?

OK, let's get on with it.

How to Use this Book

I do not recommend you just sit down and read this book. The problem is that a lot of this book describes processes that you actually need to do on your computer. If you try to read, without following along on your computer, you will get lost and not be too sure what I am talking about.

This book is a hands-on tutorial. To get the most out of it, I recommend that you sit at your computer with the book open in front of you, and follow along as you work your way through the book.

Whenever I do something on my demo site, you then do it on your own site. Don't be afraid of making mistakes; just have fun and experiment with WordPress. Mistakes can easily be undone or deleted, and anyway, most of us learn better by making a few blunders along the way.

By the end of this book, you will have a solid understanding of how WordPress works and how you can get it to do what YOU want it to do. If you then decide to take your WordPress knowledge to the next level, you'll have an excellent foundation from which to build upon.

For anyone that likes learning through video, I have a WordPress video course that you might find interesting. It's got over 8 hours of video tuition and has a Q&A section, so you can ask me questions. The course is hosted on the Udemy platform and I have a special link for all readers of this book that want to check it out. Using the link below, you can get my Udemy course for just $10:

http://ezseonews.com/wpbook

A note about UK v US English

There are some differences between UK and US English. While I try to be consistent, some errors may slip into my writing because I spend a lot of time corresponding with people in both the UK and the US. The line can blur.

Examples of this include spelling of words like optimise (UK) v optimize (US).

The difference I get the most complaints about is with collective nouns. Collective nouns refer to a group of individuals, e.g. Google. In the US, collective nouns are singular, so **Google IS** a search engine. However, in the UK, collective nouns are usually plural, so **Google ARE** a search engine.

There are other differences too. I hope that if I have been inconsistent anywhere in this book, it does not detract from the value you get from it.

Found Typos in this book?

Errors can get through proof-readers, so if you do find any typos or grammatical errors in this book, I'd be very grateful if you could let me know using this email address:

typos@ezseonews.com

What is WordPress?

WordPress is a Content Management System (CMS). That just means it is a piece of software that can help you manage and organize your content into an impressive and coherent website.

Initially, WordPress was created as a blogging tool, but over the years it has become so much more than that. Today, many WordPress driven sites look nothing like blogs (unless that's what the user wants). This is down to the flexibility of this amazing tool.

WordPress powers simple blogs, corporate websites and everything in between. Companies like Sony, the Wall Street Journal, Samsung, New York Times, Wired, CNN, Forbes, Reuters and many others, all use WordPress as part of their online presence.

WordPress is 'open source', meaning that all of its code is free to use and customize. This is one of the powers of WordPress since programmers the world over have created their own additions to this powerful publishing platform; from website templates to plugins that extend the functionality of this amazing site building tool.

Some of the features that make WordPress great

• Template system for site design means that changing the look and feel of your site is as simple as installing a new theme – literally just a few clicks of the mouse. There's a plethora of free and quality WordPress themes available.

• Plugins are pieces of code that you can download into your WordPress site to add new features and functions. There are thousands of plugins available and many are totally free.

• Once your site is set up, you can concentrate on adding great content to your site. You simply type into a text editor within the WordPress Dashboard, hit publish, and WordPress takes care of the rest.

• WordPress also has a feature called Widgets that allows the user to drag and drop "features" and place them in, for example, the sidebar. You may have a widget that allows you to display a poll to your visitors - for example. You can place that poll in the sidebar of your site by dragging the poll widget to the appropriate place. Widgets are typically used in the sidebars, but some templates allow widgets to be placed in the site footer, as well as in carefully designated areas of the homepage. We will look at widgets in much more detail later on in this book.

• WordPress can help you with the SEO (Search Engine Optimization) of your site so that it has the potential to rank higher in search engines like Google and Bing.

• WordPress can create just about any type of site, from hobby blog to e-commerce store.

WordPress.com v WordPress.org

There are actually two "flavors" of WordPress. Firstly, there is WordPress from WordPress.com, and then there is WordPress from WordPress.org.

It is vital that you understand the difference between these two.

WordPress.com

WordPress.com allows anyone to sign up to build a free "WordPress" website that WordPress.com will host on *their* servers. All you need to provide is the content for the site.

Example: Say you wanted to create a website on "educational toys for kids". You could set up a website called educationaltoysforkids.WordPress.com (assuming no one else has taken that name already).

Your website address (URL) would be:

educationaltoysforkids.WordPress.com

.. and by visiting that address in your web browser, you'd see the homepage of your site.

What you actually have is a sub-domain on the WordPress.com domain.

The main downside is that you do not own the site, WordPress.com does. One day you might go to look at your site and find that it's no longer there. You are playing by their rules.

There are also several restrictions on WordPress.com. For example, you won't be able to install any plugin you like, and you'll have a limited choice of themes/templates. You'll be unable to show any ads on your site (though WordPress.com can insert ads on your pages), which means non-profit making sites only. The interface is also greatly simplified and completely different from the one you get with the full-blown WordPress.

For these reasons, I do not recommend you create your site on WordPress.com. If you are drawn to WordPress.com because it is free, and you don't want to buy a domain and hosting while you learn to use WordPress, there is another option. Install the full-blown WordPress on your own computer!

You can then learn how to use WordPress "offline", without any additional costs. Once your website is built, you can transfer it online to a web host. If that is something you want to learn, I have a course on Udemy.com that shows you exactly how to install WordPress locally. The course is aimed at all levels of experience and assumes no prior knowledge.

You can find this, and other courses, all with considerable discounts, here:

http://ezseonews.com/udemy

Whatever you decide, this book will assume you are using the other WordPress – the one from WordPress.org.

The WordPress.com Dashboard Hack

If you just want to have a free online website and don't mind the limitations imposed by WordPress.com, I suggest you use the following Dashboard hack so you can follow along with most of this book.

This changes the simplified WordPress interface on free WordPress websites from this:

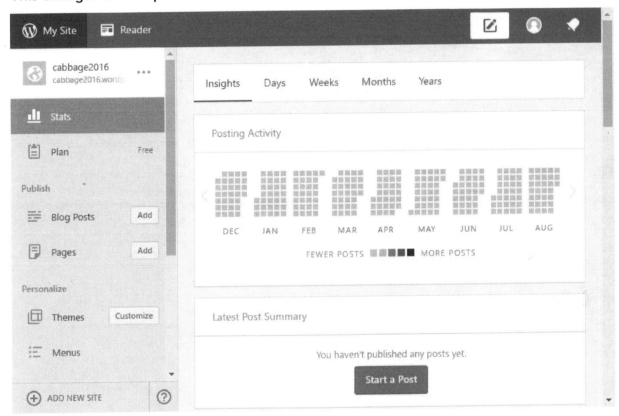

To this:

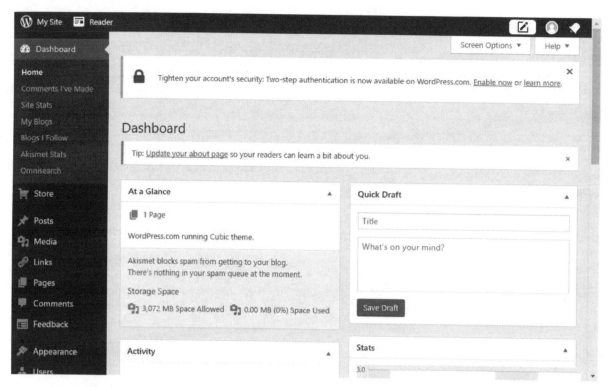

Yes, that is the exact same free WordPress.com website after applying the hack.

The dashboard now looks almost identical to the one that WordPress.org users (and this book) have, and that means you can follow most of this book as you explore and learn to use WordPress.

To apply the hack, login to your WordPress.com dashboard.

Move your mouseover **View Site** in the sidebar, and right click.

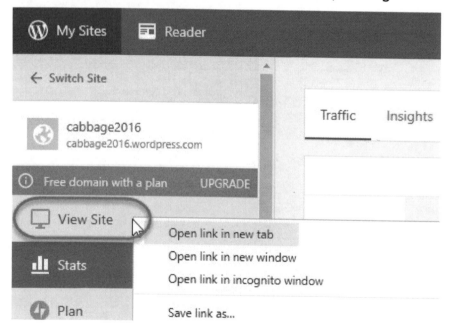

Click the **Open Link in new Tab** menu item.

This will open your site in a new browsing tab. When it opens, look at the URL in the browser address bar. Here is mine:

🔒 https://cabbage2016.wordpress.com

As you can see, the URL is a subdomain on the WordPress.com website (as discussed earlier). To access the full dashboard, add **/wp-admin** to the URL, like this:

🗋 https://cabbage2016.wordpress.com/wp-admin

.. and press the return key on your keyboard to load the new URL.

You should see this:

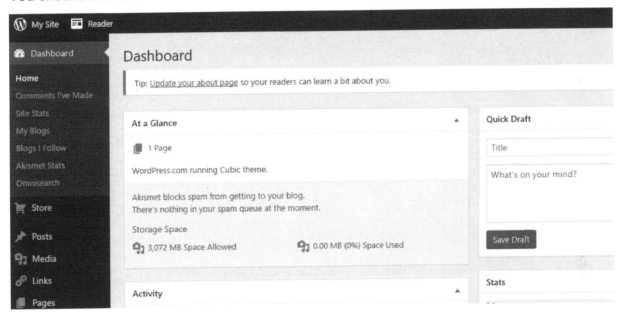

You now have a Dashboard that is very similar to the one in the WordPress.org version of WordPress. You can now follow most of the instructions in this book.

Be aware that the limitations are still present. You will be restricted in what you can do on the site, and what you can install into WordPress. That is the price you pay for using the free version. Not everything I describe in this book will be available to you.

My recommendation is to use the WordPress.org version. If you have a WordPress.com website that you want to convert to a hosted WordPress.org site, I've included a chapter at the end of this book explaining the process for moving the site.

WordPress.org

WordPress.org is a site where you can download your own copy of WordPress for free. You can then upload that copy of WordPress to any web server you like and start building a site that YOU own. You will also be able to choose whatever domain name you like, so you could call your site educationaltoysforkids.com (if it's available). Doesn't that look more professional than the options on WordPress.com?

Think of the difference between WordPress.com and WordPress.org as being like renting or owning a house. When you rent a house, there are limits to what you can do to it. You can be thrown out at any time. When you own the building outright, you can do whatever you want with it and no one can tell you how to design, decorate, or renovate *your* home.

The only disadvantages of using WordPress from WordPress.org are the costs involved. These costs are minimal though, so let's look at them.

The costs of owning your own site

So how much is a website going to cost you? As you build your site there will be optional costs – things like a website theme, autoresponder or mailing list, but these are totally optional since most things can be done for free. However, there are two costs that you cannot avoid.

The website domain

The website domain is your site's address on the internet. **Google.com** is the website domain of our favorite search engine. **CNN.com** is the domain of a popular international news service.

You will need to buy a domain for your website. We'll look at this later, but for now, let's just consider the price. Typically, a domain name will cost around $10 per year. You can sometimes get the first year for free when you buy web hosting, but once that first year is up, you'll be paying the $10 per year to keep your domain name alive.

Your domain name will be registered with a company called a registrar. It is the registrar that will collect the $10 payment every year. The registrar can be the same company that you use for your web hosting or a different company. We'll look at the pros and cons of both options later.

Website hosting

Your website needs to be "hosted" on a special type of computer called a server. Servers are connected to the internet 24/7. We call the companies that lease or rent space out on these servers "web hosts". A web host's job is to make sure their servers are up, running, and well maintained, at all times.

Since you want to create a website, you need to rent some disk space from a web host, on one of these servers. This is a monthly fee of around $5 per month (although it does vary greatly between web hosts).

As mentioned earlier, some web hosts offer a free domain name (for the first year). They can offer a free domain name because you are paying them a monthly fee for the web hosting; therefore, they get their investment back over time. To take advantage of the free domain offers, you will need to use your web host as the registrar of your domain.

The total essential costs of running your own website are:

1. $10 per year for the domain name.
2. $5 per month for the web hosting.

That´s a total of around $70 per year.

Registrar & web hosts

When you sign up with a web host, they will offer to be your domain registrar as well. The advantage is that all bills you receive are from the same company, meaning you only have to deal with ONE company.

There are disadvantages to this arrangement though, and a lot of people (including myself), prefer to keep host and registrar separate.

Potential problem: If for any reason your web host decides your website is causing them problems (i.e. they get spam complaints, or your website is using up too many system resources), they can take your site down without any warning. What happens next?

If you use a combined web host and registrar, it goes something like this:

1. Your site goes down.

2. You contact your host and they tell you that they received spam complaints about your domain.

3. They refuse to put your site back up.

4. You need to move your site to a new host, but your existing web host is the registrar and can make that difficult.

5. Your site remains down for a long period of time while you sort things out, and eventually move the site to a new host and registrar.

Time to resolve this? Weeks or months.

OK, let's see what happens if your registrar is separate from your host.

1. Your site goes down.

2. You contact your host and they tell you that they received spam complaints from your domain.

3. They refuse to put your site back up.

4. You order hosting with a different company, and copy your site to the new host.

5. You log in to your registrar account and change the name servers (don't worry about this, we'll look at it later), to the new host. This takes seconds to do.

Time to resolve this? Your site is back up within 24 hours or less, on the new web host.

This is one scenario where using a separate host and registrar is important.

Another scenario, which doesn't bear thinking about, is if your hosting company goes out of business (it does happen sometimes). What becomes of your site? Well, you probably lose it AND your domain name if your hosting company is also your registrar.

If your registrar and host are two separate companies, you'd simply get hosting somewhere else and change the name servers at your registrar. With this arrangement, your site would only be down for 24 hours or less.

Another situation that I have heard about is when a hosting company locks you out of your control panel (a login area where you can administer your domain(s)), because of a dispute over something. That means you cannot possibly move the domain to a new host because you must have access to that control panel to do it. Consequently, your domain will be down for as long as the dispute takes to resolve.

A final word of caution! I have heard horror stories of people not being able to transfer their domain out from a bad web host. Even worse than that, the domain they registered at the hosting company was not registered in their name, but in the name of the hosting company.

For all of the above reasons, when you are ready to buy hosting, please consider the separate web host and registrar that I personally use and recommend.

If you just want the easy option of using one company, use the web host I recommend. I have used them for years (sometimes as a combined host and registrar on a few sites) and never had a problem.

Recommended registrars & web hosts

Since the prices, features, etc. of web hosts can change so quickly, I have created a page on my website that lists my recommended web host and registrar.

The page also has a link to a comparative review where I show the reliability and speed of my recommended host, compared to another popular web host.

http://ezseonews.com/dwh

Tasks to complete

Read the web page above. This will give you instructions on which registrar and host to use, and how to set everything up.

1. Sign up at the recommended registrar (it's free) and buy your domain name.
2. Sign up for the recommended web hosting by following the instructions on that web page. A web host will try to get you to buy the domain from them, but you already have yours, so that web page shows how to set this all up. After following the instructions on that page, you will have bought your domain at the registrar, bought separate web hosting, and connected the two. The next step is installing WordPress.

Installing WordPress

For this, you need to login to the cPanel of your hosting. The URL, username, and password were all in the welcome email the host sent you when you signed up.

Once you are logged in, scroll down to the **Software** section, and click on the **Softaculous** app installer. Please note that depending on the version of cPanel you are using, your screen may look a little different to mine.

On the next screen, you'll see a box containing the WordPress logo. Move your mouseover it, and an **Install** button will appear:

Click the **Install** button.

At the top of the next screen, you'll see this:

Software Setup

Choose Protocol
If your site has SSL, then please choose the HTTPS protocol.

http://

Choose Domain
Please choose the domain to install the software.

harlun.co.uk

In Directory
The directory is relative to your domain and **should not exist**. e.g. To install at http://mydomain/dir/ just type **dir**. To install only in http://mydomain/ leave this empty.

In the **Choose Protocol** box, make sure **http://** is selected.

In the **"Choose Domain"** box, select the domain where you want to install WordPress.

In the **"In Directory"** box, delete the pre-filled value, leaving this empty. Failure to delete this will mean your website will be installed in a sub-folder and that is not what we want.

Next, we have these settings:

Site Settings

Site Name   My Blog

Site Description   My WordPress Blog

Enable Multisite (WPMU) ⓘ

Enter a name & description for your site. You can change these later, so don't worry too much about it.

Leave Enable Multisite (WPMU) unchecked.

Next, we have the Admin account settings:

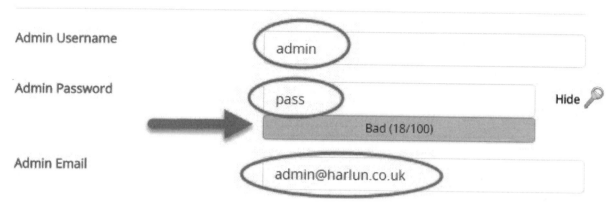

Don't use admin as your username. This is the default and will make it easier for hackers to break into your site. Change your admin username to something else using upper and lower characters, plus numbers. Also, add a strong password. You can check how strong your password is with the visual indicator underneath the password box. Use upper and lower characters, numbers, and special characters. If you are worried about remembering the password, do a Google search for password managers, and use one. They'll remember and fill passwords for you. I personally use one called Roboform, but LastPass is another good option. The username and password combination entered here will be used to login to your WordPress Dashboard, so make a note of them.

The "Admin email" box will set the admin email in your WordPress dashboard, and this will be used to notify you of events, like people leaving comments. This can be changed later.

By default, the language will be set to English, but change this if you need to.

Choose Language

Select Language

English ▼

Softaculous can install a useful plugin for you:

Select Plugins

Limit Login Attempts (Loginizer) ⓘ   ☑

Check the box next to **"Limit Login Attempts"**. This is another layer of protection against hackers.

Click the plus sign next to the **"Advanced Options"** title:

⊟ Advanced Options

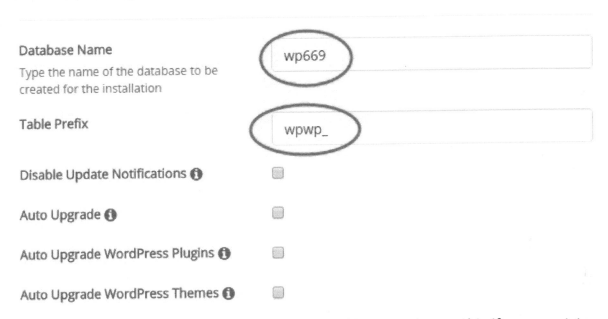

Database Name

Type the name of the database to be created for the installation

wp669

Table Prefix

wpwp_

Disable Update Notifications ⓘ   ☐

Auto Upgrade ⓘ   ☐

Auto Upgrade WordPress Plugins ⓘ   ☐

Auto Upgrade WordPress Themes ⓘ   ☐

The Database Name is set to a random value. You can change this if you want to. I personally have a lot of databases within my own hosting accounts, so prefer to use a name that would remind me what the database was being used for. E.g. I might use something like wphar22. The wp prefix would tell me it is a WordPress site, and "har" would tell me which site. The 22 at the end is just a random couple of digits to make the name more difficult to guess.

The table prefix should also be random. Some WordPress installation scripts will use wp_ by default, but hackers know this, and you should avoid it. Choose something random (Softaculous now does generate a random prefix), so you can use the default one chosen by the installation routine if you want to.

Under these two options, you have some checkboxes. These can enable/disable features in your WordPress installation. You can mouseover the little "I" buttons to see what each option does.

Finally, enter your email address at the bottom before clicking the install button. Your WordPress login details will be emailed to you at this address when WordPress is installed.

OK, once the installation has finished, you'll be shown something like this:

Congratulations, the software was installed successfully

WordPress has been successfully installed at :
http://harlun.co.uk
Administrative URL : http://harlun.co.uk/wp-admin/

We hope the installation process was easy.

The first link will load your website (currently a skeleton site created by WordPress).

The second URL listed is the Administrative URL. You can click that link to log in to the WordPress Dashboard for your site. The username and password are those that you used when filling in the Admin Details a few minutes ago.

Go check out your site

Go and look at your website in a web browser by typing the domain URL into the address bar.

You should see your WordPress site up and running. Of course, it won't have any of your content yet and it does come pre-installed with a few web pages you'll need to delete, but you should see the homepage displaying a "Hello World!" post.

Before we start learning how to configure the site, let's just log in, and then log out again, so we know how.

You should have made a note of the login URL, but if not, just add **/wp-admin** to the end of the URL, e.g.

http://mydomain.com/wp-admin

You'll be taken to the login screen:

Enter the username and password you chose when you were installing WordPress then click the "Log In" button.

I also recommend you check the "Remember Me" box so that your username and password will be automatically entered next time you log in to your Dashboard.

NOTE: If you ever forget your password, you can click the link under the login boxes to reset your password. The reset instructions will be sent to your admin email address (that's the one you entered when installing WordPress).

After logging in, you'll find yourself inside the Dashboard. You can have a look around but don't go changing anything just yet. Don't worry if it looks a little daunting in there. We'll take a tour of the Dashboard and I'll show you step-by-step, with screenshots, how to set it all up so you can have a great looking website.

Inside the Dashboard, you'll probably have notifications telling you of some plugins (and even WordPress itself) that need updating. We'll do that in a moment. For now, let's log out so you are clear on how to do that.

Move your mouseover the top right where it says "Howdy Yourname". A menu will appear:

Click the "Log Out" link.

You'll be logged out and taken back to the login screen.

Great, WordPress is installed and you know how to log in and out of the Dashboard.

In the next section, we'll take a tour of the Dashboard so you can get your bearings.

Tasks to complete

1. Install WordPress.
2. Login, have a quick look around the Dashboard, then log out.

WordPress Themes

WordPress themes control the layout, color, fonts, and general design of your site.

Every year or so, WordPress releases a new default theme. Think of these themes as demo themes, as you probably won't want to use them on your final website.

At the time of writing this, the last new theme released by WordPress was the Twenty Seventeen theme, on December 2016. There hasn't, as yet, been a Twenty Eighteen theme, but we may still see one later this year.

In my opinion, the Twenty Seventeen is not a very intuitive theme for beginners. You can, of course, install and use any theme you like. Eventually, you will want to choose a theme that is more appropriate for your website. However, while learning Wordpress, the Twenty Sixteen theme is a great one to use.

When you installed WordPress, the latest default theme plus the previous two would have been installed. You therefore currently have three themes installed. Twenty Seventeen (which is active), Twenty Sixteen and Twenty Fifteen.

To view the installed themes (and switch between them), look for the **Appearance** menu on the left, and in the popup menu that appears when you hover your mouseover, select **Themes**.

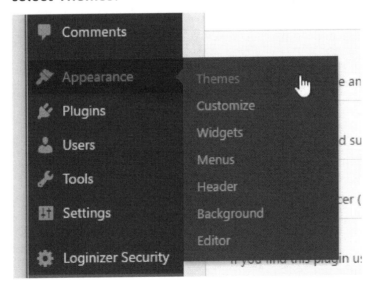

When the page loads, you'll see the installed themes.

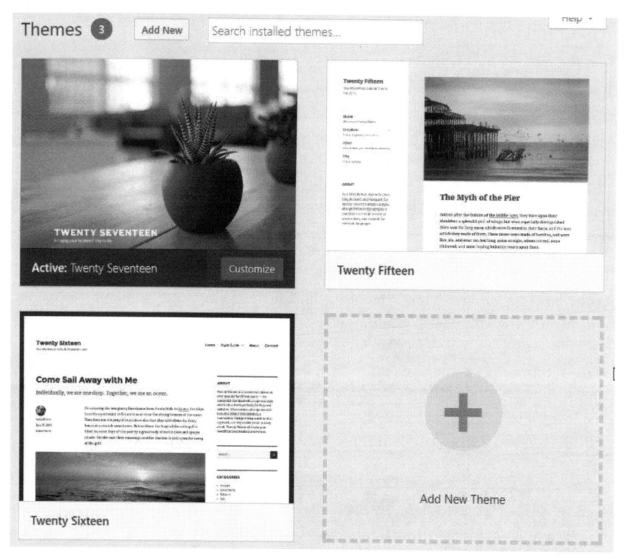

Twenty Seventeen is active.

You can see a thumbnail of each theme, hinting at what it will look like on your site. If you visit your site, you can see what the currently active theme looks like.

In the top left of your screen, you will see your website name. Place your mouse pointer over the site name and a menu drops down with one item – **Visit Site**. Click the Visit Site link. This will take you to your website as it appears to anyone that visits.

OK, click the back button on your web browser.

You'll be taken back to the Dashboard, right where you were before clicking on the visit site link.

OK, let's change to another theme.

Put your mouseover one of the other themes installed in your Dashboard and click where it says **Theme Details**. This will open a screen that displays more information about the selected theme. At the bottom, you have two buttons and a delete link.

The **Activate** button will make that theme the new active theme.

Go on, try it. Click on Activate.

Once activated, click on the visit site link again to see what your site looks like. It's very different, isn't it?

OK; click the back button in your browser to return to the theme page of the Dashboard.

Check out the third theme in the same way.

When you've seen the pre-installed themes, make the Twenty Sixteen theme the active theme again. You can take a slight shortcut here. Mouseover the Twenty Sixteen theme image and click directly on the **Activate** button. The Twenty Sixteen theme will now become active again.

Did you notice the **Live Preview** button? Mouseover an inactive theme and you'll see it:

Clicking **Live Preview** will open a preview screen showing what your site would look like with that theme, but without making it active.

You can make a theme active from the preview screen by clicking the **Save and Activate** button top left:

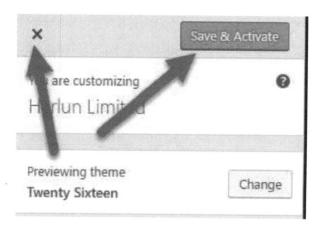

If you just want to close the preview screen without activating the theme, click the **X**.

It is a good idea to delete any themes you are not using for security reasons. Old themes may have security holes which hackers can take advantage of. At the very least, keep installed themes up to date.

Let's keep Twenty Sixteen as the active theme and delete the other two.

Move your mouseover the Twenty Fifteen theme and click the **Theme Details** button. Click the **Delete** link on the details page. You will be asked for confirmation to delete.

Repeat the process to delete the Twenty Seventeen theme. You'll be left with just the currently active Twenty Sixteen theme.

Whoops, I've deleted the wrong theme

OK, maybe you accidentally deleted the Twenty Sixteen theme and you are left with one of the others. Or maybe you've decided that you want to use the Twenty Seventeen theme after all, but it's gone. The good news is that you can easily re-install these themes (and many others) from within your Dashboard.

The first thing to do is click on **Themes** inside the **Appearance** menu. This is the screen we've been on in the previous section of this chapter. At the top, you should see an **Add New** button. Click it.

The Add Themes screen has a search box along the top to help you find themes. Enter Twenty Sixteen. As you do, you will notice the search results automatically update. The Twenty Sixteen theme should appear.

Try searching for one of the themes you deleted. If you don't have that theme installed, you can mouseover the theme thumbnail and click the install button:

If you already have the theme installed, the image of the theme will have the word **installed** written across the top.

If you click on the **Featured** link across the top of this screen, you'll see some other popular themes that are free to download. If you want to explore some of the themes from this "theme repository", knock yourself out. You won't break anything. Before you move on to the next chapter, just make sure that you have set the Twenty Sixteen theme as active, and deleted all others.

NOTE: You can use any theme you like going forward, I just recommend you use the Twenty Sixteen as you go through this book, so your screen looks the same as the screenshots in this book. You are free to change back and forth between themes whenever you like, without affecting the content or settings of your website. Think of themes as "skins". They only change the look.

In the next chapter, we are going to have a look around the WordPress Dashboard.

An overview of the Dashboard

When you log in to WordPress, you are presented with the Dashboard. This is what it looks like:

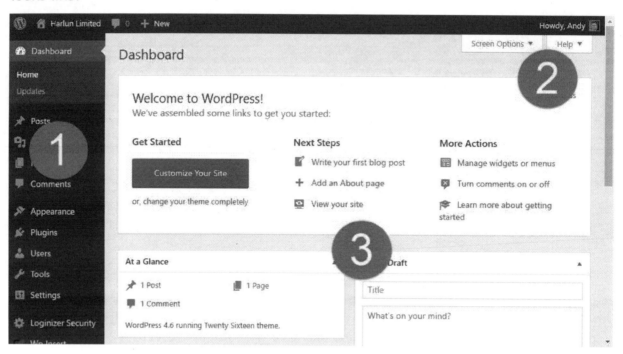

1. The Sidebar
2. Screen Options, Help, Profile & Logout
3. The Main screen

Let's look at each of these in turn.

The sidebar

The sidebar contains the Dashboard navigation menu. From this sidebar, you access all of the tools you need to administer your website.

You can add/edit content on your site, upload images, moderate comments, change your site theme, add/remove plugins, and everything else you will need to do as a website owner. We'll look at these features in detail later in the book.

Screen options, help, profile & logout

Screen Options is a drop-down menu that allows you to decide what is shown on the various screens within the Dashboard. If you click the Screen Options link, you'll see something like this:

What you see will depend on where you are in the dashboard (and the version of WordPress you are using), because the options that are shown are relevant to the current page you are viewing. For example, if you are in the section for moderating comments, the screen options will be relevant to commenting.

Columns

✓ Author   ✓ In Response To   ✓ Submitted On

Pagination

Number of items per page: 20

Apply

By changing these options, you can customize what is displayed in your Dashboard. If you don't want to see something, you simply uncheck it.

TIP: When following along with this book, if you find something missing from the screen that should be there, go in and check the screen options to ensure that it's enabled.

We will be popping into the screen options a few times in this book.

To the right of the **screen options** is a button to access WordPress help. Clicking it opens a help panel:

Overview	Welcome to your WordPress Dashboard! This is the screen you will see when you log in to your site, and gives you access to all the site management features of WordPress. You can get help for any screen by clicking the Help tab in the upper corner.	For more information:
Navigation		Documentation on Dashboard
Layout		
Content		Support Forums

Help ▲

 Dashboard

The left side of this help panel is tabbed, offering you categorized help sections. Like the screen options, the help panel is context-sensitive, so will show you the most useful help items for the Dashboard area you are currently working in.

If you need more detailed help, there are links on the right side which take you to the official WordPress documentation and support forums.

Finally, in this area of the Dashboard screen, if you place your mouseover the "Howdy Yourname" top right, a panel opens:

NOTE: Mine shows a photo of myself. I'll show you how & why later when we look at Gravatars in the User Profile section.

This menu gives you a direct link to edit your profile (which we will fill out later) and a link to log out of your WordPress Dashboard. Whenever you finish a session in the WordPress Dashboard, it's always a good idea to log out.

The main screen

This is where all the work takes place. What you see in the main screen area will depend on where you are in the Dashboard. For example, if you are in the comments section, the main screen area will list all the comments people have made on your site. If you are in the appearance section of your Dashboard, the main screen section will show you the theme/template of your site. If you are adding or editing a post, the main screen area will have everything you need to add/edit a post.

Tasks to complete

1. Go in and explore the Dashboard to familiarize yourself with the system.
2. Go and check out the pre-installed WordPress Themes.
3. Delete all inactive themes, for security reasons. You should be left with just the Twenty Sixteen theme.
4. Click on a few of the menu items in the left navigation column and then open the screen options to see what's there. See how the options are related to the page you are viewing in the Dashboard?
5. Have a look at the help options – the forum and the other WordPress documentation. You won't need any of that now, but it is a good idea to be familiar with these options just in case you get stuck in the future.

Cleaning out the preinstalled stuff

When you install WordPress, it installs a few default items like the "Hello World" post you saw on the homepage earlier. In addition to that post, there is a "Sample page", a comment, some widgets and a few plugins.

NOTE: WordPress allows you to create two types of "article" - posts and pages. Don't worry about the differences just yet as we'll look at them later.

In this chapter, we'll look at deleting the pre-installed post, comment, page, and widgets.

Deleting the "Hello World" post

If you visit your site homepage, you'll see that the "Hello World" post is displayed front and center.

To delete the post, we need to use the "Posts" menu from the sidebar navigation.

You can either move your mouseover the word **Posts** and select **All Posts** from the popup menu, like this:

Or you can click the word **Posts**, and the sub-menu will become integrated into the left sidebar. You can then click the **All Posts** link:

This will open a table of all posts on your site:

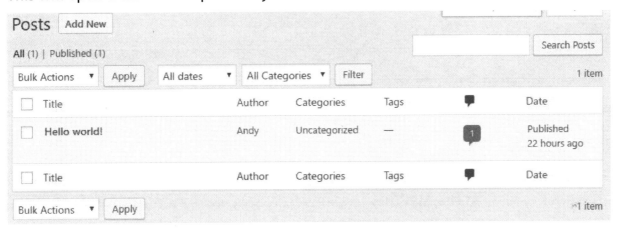

Something to try...

Open the **Screen Options** top right, and uncheck/check some of the boxes to see how it affects what you see on your screen.

Try out the **Excerpt View** in the **View Mode** Section (hint: You will need to click the Apply button for that to take effect).

OK; now you've had some fun, let's delete the Hello World post.

Move your mouseover the title of the post. A menu appears underneath:

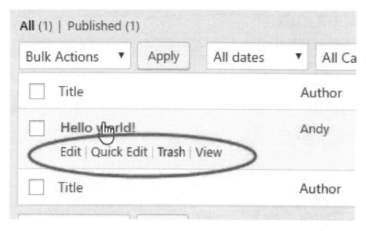

This menu allows you to:

1. Edit the post
2. Quick Edit - which allows you to edit the title, category, etc., but not the content of the post.
3. Move the post to Trash (i.e. delete it).
4. View the post – which will open the post in the current browser window.

We want to delete the post, so click on the "Trash" link. The screen will refresh, and the post will be gone.

If you accidentally delete a post, don't worry. It will remain in the trash until you empty the trash. I actually want to keep the "Hello World!" post on my site so that I can use it later in the book. Let's undelete the post.

To do this, you go to the **All Posts** screen (which is where we are right now) and look for the **Trash** link above the table of posts.

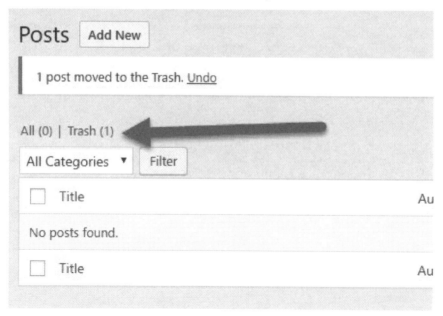

There is a (1) next to the Trash link. That means there is one item in the trash (my Hello Word post). If you click on the Trash link, you'll be taken to the trash bin where you can see all the posts that were sent to there.

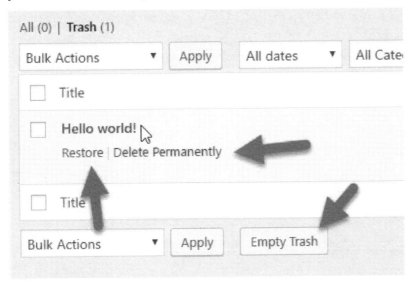

If you mouse-over the post title, you'll get another popup menu. This one allows you to restore the post (i.e. undelete it), or delete it permanently.

If you have a lot of posts in the trash and you want to delete them all, click the "Empty Trash" button at the bottom.

NOTE: When WordPress created the "Hello World!" post, it also added a demo comment to the post. When you deleted the post, the comment was also deleted because it belonged to that post. When you undelete (restore) a post, any comments that were deleted with the post are also restored.

I am going to click on the **Restore** link to undelete the Hello World post and comment. You can do the same if you wish. You know how to delete it when you decide you want to.

Deleting the sample page

In the sidebar navigation of your Dashboard, open the **Pages** menu and click on **All Pages**.

Like the posts section, this will bring up a list of all pages on the site. Mouseover the Sample page title, and click the **Trash** link underneath it.

As with posts, pages remain in the trash until it's emptied, and can, therefore, be restored if required.

Deleting widgets

WordPress pre-configured your website with a number of widgets in the sidebar of your website. You can see them if you look at your website:

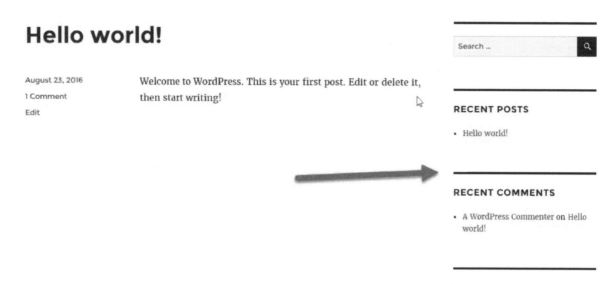

Those are widgets on the right. Let's delete them.

In your Dashboard, move your mouseover the **Appearance** menu, and click on **Widgets**:

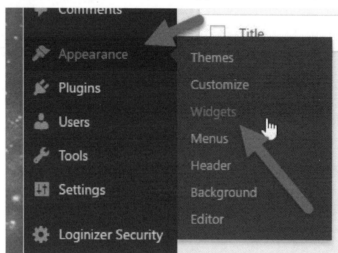

This will take you to the widget screen:

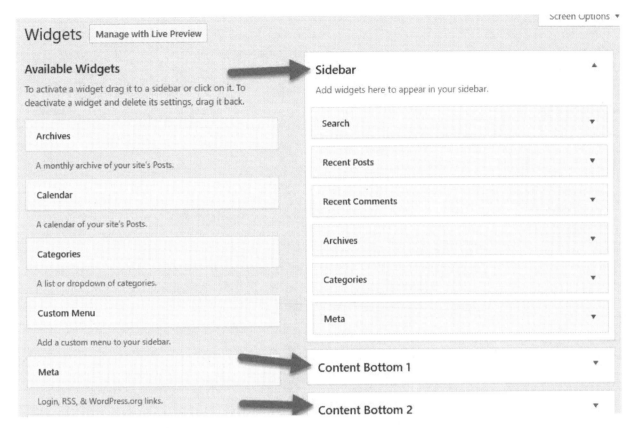

The screen is split into two sections.

On the left, you'll see the **Available Widgets**.

On the right, you have "widgetized areas". These are areas on your web page that can hold widgets. For example, the top widgetized area is the Sidebar (this section is opened in my screenshot to show 6 widgets in the sidebar area). Any widgets in this area will appear in the sidebar on the website.

You can insert widgets into the widgetized areas of your site by dragging and dropping them onto the corresponding area on the right. Be aware that different themes have different widgetized areas, so if you are not using the Twenty Sixteen theme from WordPress, you will be seeing something a little different on the right-hand side.

The Twenty Sixteen theme also has two other widgetized areas called **Content Bottom 1** and **Content Bottom 2**. These correspond to areas on your web page, but where?

The easiest way to find out is to drag a widget into each area and see where they appear on the Hello World post.

Click and drag a Calendar Widget, dropping it in the Content Bottom 1 widgetized area. Under the title of the widget, type Content Bottom 1.

In the Content Bottom 2 area, drag and drop a Text widget. When you drop it, there is space for you to add a title and some text.

35

Here is mine:

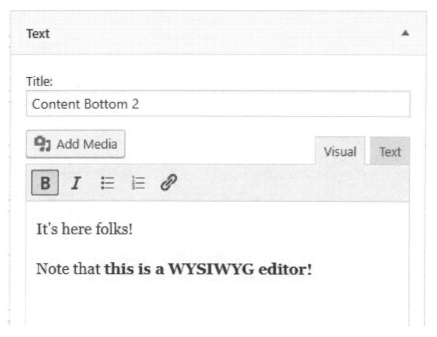

Once you've typed something in, click the Save button at the bottom of the text widget.

OK; now go and visit your website.

You won't see the calendar or text widget on the homepage. We need to visit a post (don't worry, this will all become clear later in the book). To visit the Hello World post, click on the Hello World title on your homepage. As you move your mouseover the title, it should change color (indicating it is a link). After clicking the title, you'll land on the Hello World post, and if you scroll down, you will see the Content Bottom 1 & 2 widgetized areas at the bottom of the screen (after the post and comments section).

January 2018

M	T	W	T	F	S	S
1	2	3	4	5	6	7
8	9	10	11	12	13	14
15	16	17	18	19	20	21
22	23	24	25	26	27	28
29	30	31				

CONTENT BOTTOM 2

It's here folks!

Note that **this is a WYSIWYG editor!**

Widgetized areas are simply pre-defined areas on your webpage that allow you to insert something (in the form of a widget).

All WordPress themes are different and will provide you with their own unique widgetized areas. Common areas include the footer, sidebar and even header of the web page. The best way to find out where each widgetized area is on the website is to consult the documentation that came with your theme or just add a widget and see where it appears.

Let's clear out the pre-installed widgets, and those two we just added.

WordPress installed several widgets into the "Main Sidebar" area of your site.

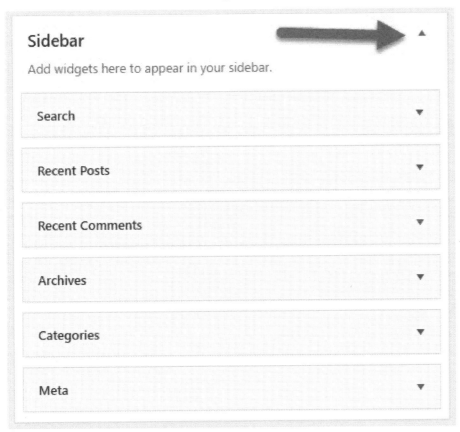

You can open each widgetized area using the arrow to the right of the area title.

In the sidebar, you can see widgets called Search, recent posts, recent comments, archives, categories, and Meta.

Each installed Widget has a small downward-pointing arrow next to it on the right. Click this arrow to open the settings for that particular widget:

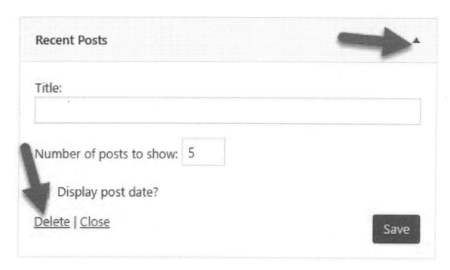

You'll see a couple of options available for this "Recent Posts" widget. You can enter a title (leaving this blank will use the default title for the widget, in this case, "Recent Posts"). You can also specify how many posts to show. This one is set to 5.

To delete the widget, click the **Delete** link bottom left.

The widget will disappear from the Main Sidebar area. Repeat to delete all the other widgets in the sidebar (and the two we added to the other areas). The only one I am leaving for now is the **Meta** widget. This gives me an easy link to log in to my site from the homepage, so I'll keep it there for now while I am working on the site. You can do the same if you wish.

OK, we are done cleaning out WordPress.

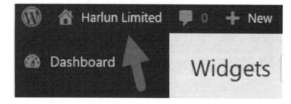

Go and visit your site:

Harlun Limited
Company Website

Hello world!

META

August 23, 2016

Welcome to WordPress. This is your first post. Edit or delete it, then start writing!

1 Comment

Edit

- Site Admin
- Log out
- Entries RSS
- Comments RSS
- WordPress.org

Harlun Limited / Proudly powered by WordPress

If you deleted the Hello World post, you will just see a message saying, "Nothing Found". In my screenshot, the Hello World post is shown on the homepage, and you can see the Meta widget I left in the right sidebar.

Tasks to complete

1. Delete the Hello World post and then restore it.
2. Delete the pre-installed Page.
3. Explore the various widgets that WordPress has given you. Drag & drop them into widgetized areas to see what they look like on your website, and where they appear. Note that some widgets may show nothing at all. This is simply because there is nothing to show until there is some data they can work with.

Dashboard updates

WordPress makes it easy for us to know when there are updates. It shows a number in a red circle next to the **Updates** menu. That number tells you how many updates are available, in my case, 5!

Available updates can include plugins, themes and WordPress itself!

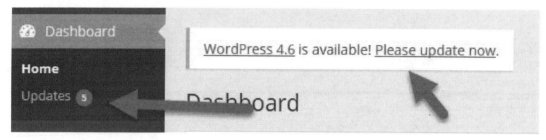

Click on the **Updates** menu item.

At the top of the screen, you'll see a notification whenever there is a new update to WordPress itself. Click on the **Please update now** link to update WordPress if necessary. Occasionally these WordPress updates will require you to click a button or two, e.g. to update the database:

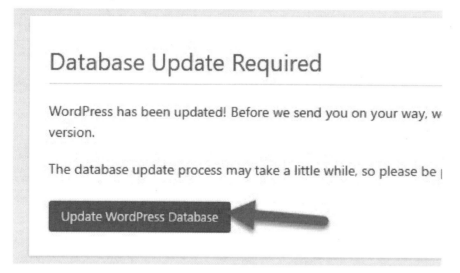

Just follow all screen prompts, and the update will complete and take you back to the Dashboard.

Back on the **Updates** screen, WordPress will be up-to-date but there are plugins that need updating:

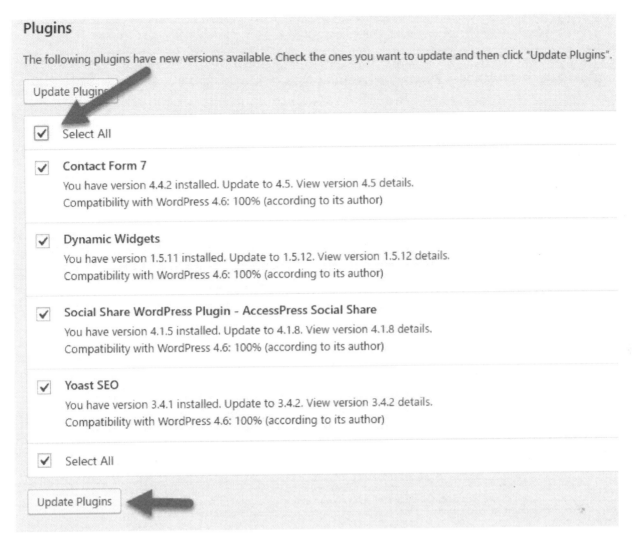

Plugins

The following plugins have new versions available. Check the ones you want to update and then click "Update Plugins".

Update Plugins

☑ Select All

☑ **Contact Form 7**
You have version 4.4.2 installed. Update to 4.5. View version 4.5 details.
Compatibility with WordPress 4.6: 100% (according to its author)

☑ **Dynamic Widgets**
You have version 1.5.11 installed. Update to 1.5.12. View version 1.5.12 details.
Compatibility with WordPress 4.6: 100% (according to its author)

☑ **Social Share WordPress Plugin - AccessPress Social Share**
You have version 4.1.5 installed. Update to 4.1.8. View version 4.1.8 details.
Compatibility with WordPress 4.6: 100% (according to its author)

☑ **Yoast SEO**
You have version 3.4.1 installed. Update to 3.4.2. View version 3.4.2 details.
Compatibility with WordPress 4.6: 100% (according to its author)

☑ Select All

Update Plugins

You can update all the plugins by checking the boxes next to each one (the **Select All** checkbox will check them all with a single click), and then click the **Update Plugins** button.

Once the plugin updates have been completed, WordPress will ask you where you want to go next:

All updates have been completed.

Return to Plugins page | Return to WordPress Updates page

If there are still updates to perform, click the link to return to WordPress updates.

If there are no more updates available, you can click on any of the sidebar menus to go wherever you want.

In the next chapter, we will configure WordPress so that it is ready for our content.

Tasks to complete

1. Check to see if there are any updates needing your attention. If there are, go and update everything. Whenever you log in to your Dashboard, if there are updates pending, it is a good idea (for security reasons) to update them immediately.

WordPress Settings

In the sidebar, you'll see an item labeled **Settings**.

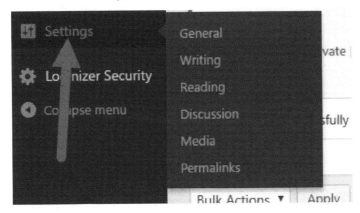

Within **Settings,** there are a number of items. Let's look at each one in turn and configure things as we go through.

General Settings

The General settings page defines some of the basic website settings.

At the top of the screen, the first few settings look like this:

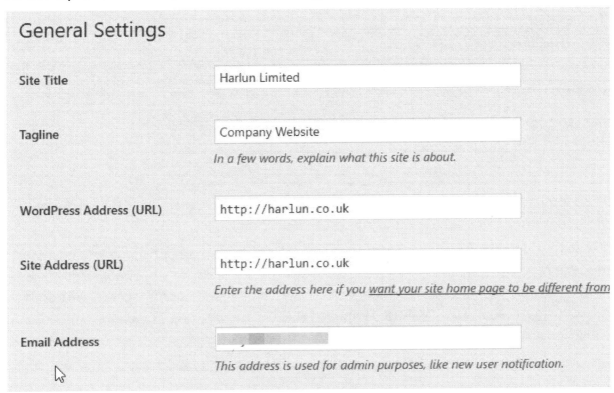

The information on the General Settings page was filled in when you installed WordPress, and there is probably no reason to change anything.

Right at the top is the Site Title. This is usually the same as the domain name but doesn't have to be.

Under the title is the Tagline. On some themes, the tagline is displayed in the site header right under the site name. The Twenty Sixteen theme is one theme that does this. Go and check out your website and you'll see the tagline sitting right underneath the site title.

You can use the tagline to give your visitors more information about your website. A tagline may be your website's "catchphrase", slogan, mission statement, or just a very brief, one-sentence description.

The next two fields on this settings page are the **WordPress Address (URL)** and the **Site Address (URL)**. The WordPress Address is the URL where WordPress is installed. Since we installed it in the root folder of this site, the WordPress Address is identical to the Site Address.

NOTE: Advanced users might want to install WordPress in a folder on their server, yet still have the site appear as if it were in the root folder. They can achieve this by using the WordPress Address (URL) field. Confused? Don't be. You won't be doing this.

Next on this setting page is the email address. This is very important as you'll get all notifications sent to this email address. Make sure you use a valid email that you check frequently.

Lower down this General Setting page are these options:

Membership	☐ Anyone can register
New User Default Role	Subscriber ▼

The **Membership** option allows visitors to sign up on your site, with their role being defined in the **New User Default Role** drop-down box.

E.g. you could allow visitors to sign up as subscribers or maybe contributors to your site. This can open up a whole can of security worms, so I don't advise you enable this option. If you want to create a "membership" site, use a dedicated, secure WordPress membership plugin, like Wishlist Member (which can turn any WordPress site into a fully-fledged membership site).

The rest of the settings on this page allow you to set your time zone, date and time formats.

The timezone is used to correctly timestamp posts on your site. Since we'll look at how you can schedule your posts into the future, the correct time zone will ensure your posts are going out on the intended dates and times.

Select the date and time format you use.

You can also set the day you use for the start of the week. This will be used if you use a calendar widget in your sidebar. If you choose Monday as the start of the week, then Monday will be the first column in the calendar.

If you make any changes to the settings on the General Settings tab, make sure you save the changes when you are finished.

Writing

The writing settings control the user interface you see when you are adding/editing posts. Let's look at the options.

Here are the first two:

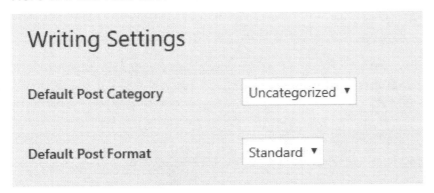

The **Default Post Category** is the category that a post will be assigned to if you don't manually select a category. We haven't set up any categories yet. WordPress set one up for us during installation, called **Uncategorized**, so that is the current default. We'll rename that to something more useful when we look at categories later in the book.

The **Default Post Format** is the default layout/appearance of the posts you add to your site. This is controlled by the template you are using, with different templates having different options. Here are the post formats in Twenty Sixteen (found on the edit post screen):

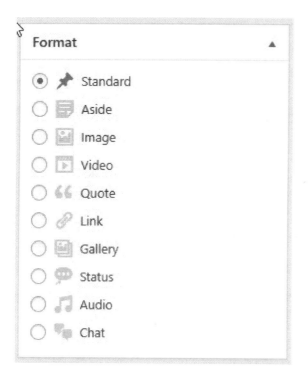

Each of these will modify how a post looks, so I recommend you use the Standard option for the default value, and then change the format on a post by post basis if needed.

Here are the next few settings:

The Post via e-mail can be set up so that you can post content to your site by sending it in as an email. This is beyond the scope of this book.

The final setting on this page is important. It's the update services:

Update Services

When you publish a new post, WordPress automatically notifies the follow
Codex. Separate multiple service URLs with line breaks.

```
http://rpc.pingomatic.com/
```

Save Changes

Basically, every time you post new content on your site, a message is sent to all "services" in this list (currently just one) to let them know there is new content. They will then typically come over to your site to index the content.

This list helps your content get noticed and included more quickly in the search engines. WordPress installs just one service, but I recommend you add more.

Do a search on Google for "WordPress Ping List" and you'll find ready-made lists created by other webmasters. Just find a list and paste it into the box. Save your changes before moving to the next settings page.

Reading

The reading settings define how your visitors will see certain aspects of your site.

There are only a few settings here, but they are important.

Reading Settings

Blog pages show at most   [10] posts

Syndication feeds show the
most recent   [10] items

For each article in a feed, show   ● Full text

                                    ○ Summary

Search Engine Visibility   [ ] Discourage search engines from indexing this site

                                 It is up to search engines to honor this request.

[Save Changes]

Some pages on your site like the category, tag, and homepage, can show lists of posts. **Blog pages show at most**, defines how many posts appear on those pages.

This setting will make more sense when you start adding content to your site. You'll then be able to see what WordPress does with that content as you add it.

Here is an example. If you have a category on your site called "types of roses", WordPress will create a category page called "Types of Roses". That page will list all posts in that category. If you have 15 articles, each describing a different rose, then WordPress will create two category pages to hold those articles (assuming you left the default set to 10 per page). The first category page will have links to the first 10, and the second will list the remaining 5.

I recommend you leave the setting at the default 10.

Syndication feeds show the most recent, refers to your website's RSS feed. Every WordPress site has an RSS feed (in fact it has many RSS feeds). An RSS feed is just a list of the most recent articles with a link and a description of each post. This setting allows you to define how many of your most recent posts appear in the feed. Again, I recommend 10. We'll look at RSS feeds in more detail later.

For each article in a feed, show, defines what content is shown in the feed. If you select "Full Text", then the complete articles are included in the feed. This can make your feed very long, but also give spammers a chance to steal your content with tools designed to scrape RSS feeds and post the content to their own sites.

I recommend you change this setting to Summary. That way only a short summary of each post will be displayed in the feed, which is far less appealing to spammers and easier on the eye for those who genuinely follow your active RSS feeds.

Search Engine Visibility allows you to effectively hide your site from the search engines. If you are working on a site that you don't want the search engines to find, you can check this box.

I allow search engines to visit and index my site from day 1. Yes, the search engines will find content that is not finished, but that's OK because they'll come back and check the site periodically to pick up changes.

Whether you block the search engines now or not is up to you. Just remember that if you do, your site won't start appearing in the search engines until you unblock them.

I recommend you leave this setting unchecked.

Make sure you click the **Save Changes** button at the bottom if you've edited the settings on the screen.

NOTE: If you have created a WordPress Page, there will be another section at the top of these settings which defines what is displayed on the homepage:

The default setting is **Your Latest Posts**. This will display the most recent posts on your homepage. The number of posts displayed on your homepage is determined by whatever you have the **Blog pages show at most** set to. Since the default is 10, that means your last 10 posts will appear on your homepage.

However, it is possible to set up the homepage like a more traditional website, with a single article forming the basis of the homepage content. You can do this in WordPress by creating a WordPress PAGE that contains your homepage article. You then select **A Static Page** from the options and choose the page from the **Homepage** drop-down list. We'll do this later.

Discussion

The discussion settings are related to comments that visitors may leave at the end of your posts. There are a few settings we need to change from the default.

Here are the first few settings in the discussion options:

Default article settings	☑ Attempt to notify any blogs linked to from the article
	☑ Allow link notifications from other blogs (pingbacks and trackbacks) on new articles
	☑ Allow people to post comments on new articles
	(These settings may be overridden for Individual articles.)

Attempt to notify any blogs linked to from the article should be left checked. Whenever you write an article and link to another site, WordPress will try to notify that site that you have linked to them. WordPress does this by sending what is called a Ping. Pings will show up in the comment system of the receiving blog and can be approved like a comment. If it is approved, that Pingback will appear near the comments section on that blog, giving you a link back to your site.

NOTE: Any website can turn pingbacks off. If a ping is sent to a site where pingbacks are OFF, then it won't appear in their comment system.

Here are some example pingbacks published on a web page:

3 Responses to *Men's Health Week Proclamations*

1. Pingback: health » Blog Archive » Focus on Men's Health Week This Father's Day : Healthymagination

2. Pingback: Focus on Men's Health Week This Father's Day : Healthymagination – health

3. Pingback: Focus on Men's Health Week This Father's Day : Healthymagination – men health

Each pingback is a link back to a website that has linked to this webpage.

The next option - **Allow link notifications from other blogs (pingbacks and trackbacks)** allows you to turn pingbacks and trackbacks (trackbacks are very similar to pingbacks) off. If you uncheck this, you will not receive pingbacks or trackbacks.

Should you check it or not?

Well, it's always nice to see when a site is linking to your content. However, there is a technique used by spammers to send fake trackbacks & pingbacks to your site. They are trying to get you to approve their trackback so that your site will then link to theirs.

Personally, I uncheck this option, but if you do leave it checked, then never approve a trackback or pingback. They are nearly always spam!

Allow people to post comments on new articles should remain checked. It is important that you let your visitors comment on your site's content. A lot of people disable this because they think moderating comments is too much work, but from an SEO point of view, search engines love to see active discussions on websites. Leave it checked!

The next section of options is shown below:

Other comment settings	☑ Comment author must fill out name and email
	☐ Users must be registered and logged in to comment
	☐ Automatically close comments on articles older than `14` days
	☑ Enable threaded (nested) comments `5` ▼ levels deep
	☐ Break comments into pages with `50` top level comments per page and the
	`last` ▼ page displayed by default
	Comments should be displayed with the `older` ▼ comments at the top of each page

Leave these at their default value (shown above).

The options are self-explanatory but let's go through them quickly.

The first option requires commenters to fill in a name and email. This is very important and often a good indicator of legitimate/spam comments. Spammers tend to fill the name field with keywords (for SEO purposes), whereas legitimate commenters are more likely to use a real name. The email is nice too, so you can follow up with commenters.

The second item should remain unchecked because we do not allow visitors to register and login to our site. We do want *all* visitors to have the option of leaving a comment though.

The third option allows you to close the comment sections on posts after a certain number of days. I like to leave comments open indefinitely as you never know when someone will find your article and want to have their say. However, if you want to cut back on spam comments, then close comments after a reasonable length of time, say 30 days.

Nested comments should be enabled. This allows people to engage in discussions within the comments section, with replies to previous comments "nested" underneath the comment they are replying to. Here is an example showing how nested comments appear on my site:

Marshall says:

18/6/2013 at 06:06

I purchased the KD Suite tonight because Andy does good videos. I could have purchased directly from Guindon since I had purchased other products from him. However the productpay.com fulfillment system absolutely sucks. I did not get my bonus downloads because the bonus page got closed before I could get all the membership BS set up and then back to the download page. As opposed to other systems such as JVZoo where you get download information and login information from them, productpay sucks your money and does not much else. And they have no way to contact them without setting up another account with them just to send a support ticket. Plus they hide behind Domains by Proxy owned by Godaddy.com. What kind of legitimate fulfillment company needs to hide their registration information. I have contacted Guindon directly about this and I am sure Dave will make it right. But what a pain in the butt process. If you purchase from productpay.com just be forwarned to download everything first then worry about any membership BS.

You can bet none of Dr Andy's membership sites worked like this. I know because I bought a lot of his products.

Reply

Andy Williams says:

18/6/2013 at 07:59

Totally agree Marshall. They really could do a lot better. Also, thanks for your loyalty 🙂

Reply

Marshall says:

18/6/2013 at 09:56

Andy You are welcome. Your software has always worked out of the box without a lot of bugs. And the very few that came up you fixed right away. Your courses were right on the mark too. For what it is worth, Dave got about 5 emails from me tonight so maybe he will rethink his choice of fulfillment companies.

The KD Bestseller analyzer was worth the hassle of getting it and getting it activated. I have played with it for about 3 hours tonight. My niche I was writing in is a real loser for making money. The fiction, adventure, romance are really hot now. I have one more herb book to do

You can see that replies to the previous comment are nested underneath them, making it clear that the comments are part of a conversation.

The last two options in this section relate to how comments are displayed on the page. If you want, comments can be spread across multiple pages, with say 50 comments per page (default). However, I leave this option unchecked so that all comments for an article appear on the same page. If you find that you get hundreds of comments per article (which will slow down the load time of the page), you might want to enable this option so pages load faster.

The final option in this section allows you to show older or newer comments at the top of the comments section.

I prefer comments listed in the order in which they are submitted, as that makes more sense. Therefore, leave the setting as "older".

The next section of these settings is shown below:

Email me whenever	☑ Anyone posts a comment
	☑ A comment is held for moderation
Before a comment appears	☑ Comment must be manually approved
	☐ Comment author must have a previously approved comment

You can choose to be notified via email when someone posts a comment, and/or when a comment is held for moderation. The way I suggest you set up your site is that all comments are held for moderation, so effectively, those two options are the same thing.

Check one or other of these two options so you know when there are comments waiting for approval. When you get an email notification, you can then log in to your Dashboard and either approve the comment (so it goes live on your site) or send it to trash if it's blatant spam.

The second two options shown above relate to when a comment can appear on the site. Check the box next to **Comment must be manually approved**. This will mean ALL comments must be approved by you before appearing on the site.

The second option will allow you to auto-approve comments by commenters that have had previous comments approved (i.e. trusted commenters). I recommend you leave this option unchecked for reasons I will mention in a moment. If you did want to use this feature, the first option would need to be unchecked.

So why do I not recommend this option?

A hacking technique (zero-day exploit) targeted sites that were set up to auto-approve comments once a first comment was approved. Hackers would get a harmless comment approved, and then post a comment that contained malicious JavaScript. The JavaScript comment would never be manually approved on its own, but with the first comment already approved, it would get automatic approval.

The comment moderation settings are not important to us since all our comments are moderated.

Comment Moderation

Hold a comment in the queue if it contains [2] or more links. (A common characteristic of comment spam is a large number of hyperlinks.)

When a comment contains any of these words in its content, name, URL, email, or IP, it will be held in the moderation queue. One word or IP per line. It will match inside words, so "press" will match "WordPress".

If you do not want to manually moderate all comments, you can use these settings to automatically add a comment to the moderation queue IF it has a certain number of links in it (default is 2), OR the comment contains a word that is listed in the big box.

The Comment Blacklist box allows you to set up a blacklist to automatically reject comments that meet the criteria listed here.

Comment Blacklist

When a comment contains any of these words in its content, name, URL, email, or IP, it will be put in the trash. One word or IP per line. It will match inside words, so "press" will match "WordPress".

Essentially any comment that contains a word or URL listed in this box, or comes from an email address or IP address listed in this box, will automatically be sent to the trash.

That means you can set up your blacklist with "unsavory" words, email addresses, URLs or IP addresses of known spammers, and you'll never see those comments in your moderation queue. The comment blacklist can significantly cut down on your comment moderation, so I suggest you do a search on Google for **WordPress comment blacklist** and use a list that someone else has already put together (you'll find a few). Just copy and paste their list into the box and save the settings.

The final section of the discussion options is related to Avatars:

Avatars

An avatar is an image that follows you from weblog to weblog appearing beside your name when you comment on ava
Here you can enable the display of avatars for people who comment on your site.

Avatar Display	☑ Show Avatars
Maximum Rating	◉ G — Suitable for all audiences
	○ PG — Possibly offensive, usually for audiences 13 and above
	○ R — Intended for adult audiences above 17
	○ X — Even more mature than above

An Avatar is an image/photo that appears next to the commenter's name.

I think it is nice to see who is leaving comments, so I recommend you leave Avatars on (first setting).

For most websites, you should have the maximum rating set to G. This will then hide any Avatars that are not suitable for your viewers. Avatars are assigned ratings when you create them over at Gravatar.com, so this rating system is only as good as the honesty of the person creating the avatar.

The final setting allows you to define the default action if someone does not have an Avatar set up for their email address.

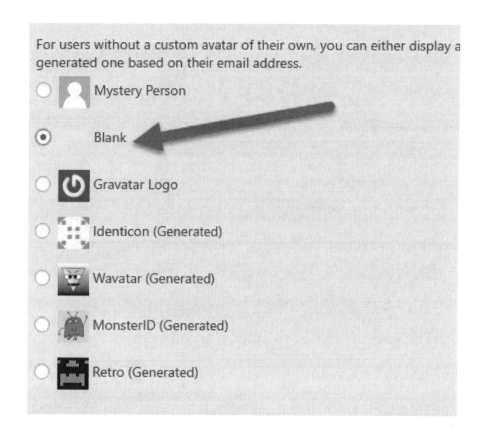

For users without a custom avatar of their own, you can either display a generated one based on their email address.

○   Mystery Person

◉   Blank

○   Gravatar Logo

○   Identicon (Generated)

○   Wavatar (Generated)

○   MonsterID (Generated)

○   Retro (Generated)

I recommend you select **Blank** so that no avatar is shown. This is because Avatar images need to load with the page. Any page with a lot of comments will have a lot of Avatars to load, and this can slow down the load speed of the page. Why slow it further with "Mystery Man" avatars when the commenter doesn't have an avatar set up?

When you have finished with these settings, save the changes.

Media

The media settings relate to images and other media that you might insert into your site.

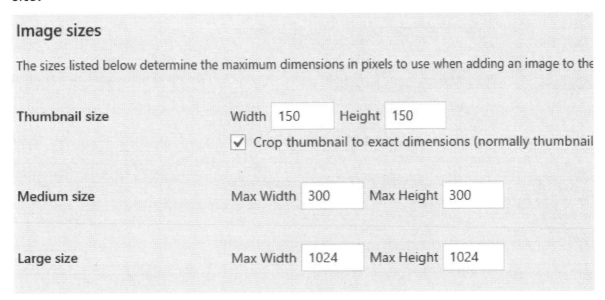

These first few settings allow you to define the maximum dimensions for the thumbnail, medium, and large images. You can leave these at their default settings.

The final option asks whether you want your uploaded images to be organized into month and year based folders.

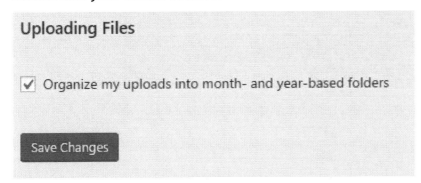

I'd recommend you leave this checked, just so your images are organized into dates on your server. It can help you find the images later if you need to.

Permalinks

The final settings are the permalinks. These define how the URLs (web addresses) are structured for your web pages.

We want the URLs on our site to help visitors and search engines, so I recommend they contain both the category and filename:

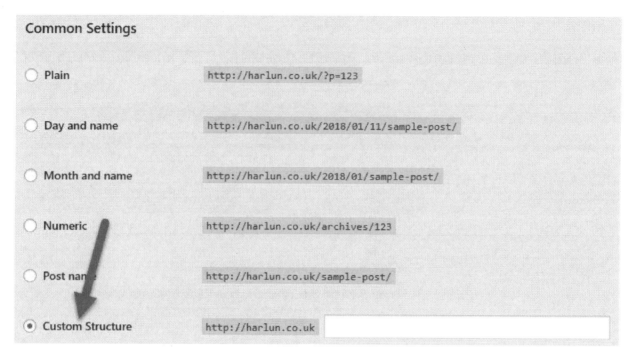

Select the **Custom Structure** radio button at the bottom of the list and then click on the %category% button, followed by the %postname% button:

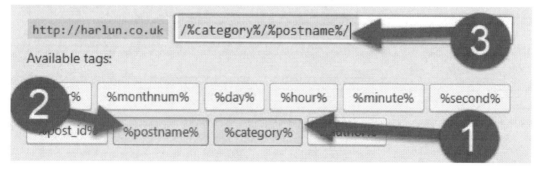

Watch how the permalink structure is automatically written as your custom structure.

Save the changes.

The URLs on your site will now look like this:

http://mydomain/category/post-name

The last two options on this settings page are shown below:

Optional

If you like, you may enter custom structures for your category and tag URLs here. For example, using `to` would make your category links like `http://harlun.co.uk/topics/uncategorized/`. If you leave th used.

Category base

Tag base

Save Changes

I would leave these two boxes empty.

When WordPress creates a category page or a tag page, the URL will include the word "category" or "tag".

For example:

http://mydomain.com/**category**/roses/

.. might be the URL of a category page listing my posts on Roses, and

http://mydomain.com/**tag**/red

.. might be a tag page listing all posts on my site that were tagged with the word "red".

If you enter a word into the category base or tag base, the URLs will contain the words you enter here, rather than the default "category" or "tag".

Having keywords in your URL can be helpful, BUT, with Google on the warpath against web spammers, I would not even consider entering a category base or tag base. Leave those boxes empty.

Congratulations, you have now set up your main WordPress Settings.

Tasks to complete

1. Go through each of the items inside the settings menu and make the changes described in this chapter.

RSS feeds

We mentioned RSS feeds earlier when setting up the Reading options.

RSS feeds are an important part of your WordPress website, so I wanted to spend a little more time on this.

RSS stands for **R**eally **S**imple **S**yndication (or **R**ich **S**ite **S**ummary). An RSS feed lists information about the most recent posts on your site. This information is typically the title of the post (which links to the article on your website), and a description of it, which can be short or the entire piece.

The RSS feed is an XML document that would be difficult to read without special software, but XML is the perfect "language" to store this information.

Most web browsers can read RSS feeds and show their content as readable text. Here is an RSS feed from a website on "juicing", as displayed in my copy of Google Chrome:

Current Feed Content

Measuring heat with the Scoville Scale
Posted: Fri, 12 Oct 2012 18:20:17 +0000
Chili heat is measured on the Scoville scale.

The World's Hottest Chili
Posted: Thu, 11 Oct 2012 15:01:00 +0000
What happens when you eat the world's hottest chili pepper? Watch this video and find out.

Health benefits of the Jalapeno Chili pepper
Posted: Thu, 11 Oct 2012 10:32:57 +0000
I love tabasco sauce. There is something about the spicy taste that is addictive. Since I found out about the health benefits of capsaicin in chilies, I have been enjoying even more tabasco and started growing my own chilies.

Antioxidant 2011 Championships
Posted: Mon, 08 Oct 2012 21:11:00 +0000
Some interesting experiments with Asdtaxanthin. The second experiment with egg yolks is quite incredible.

You can see the summaries of the last 4 posts on my site.

Each entry has the title of the post which is hyperlinked to the article on the site. Under the title is the date and time of the post and then a short description under that.

This is much easier for humans to read than the raw XML code. Here is the raw XML for just the first item in that RSS feed:

```
<feedburner:feedburnerHostname xmlns:feedburner="
http://rssnamespace.org/feedburner/ext/1.0">http://feedburner.google.com
</feedburner:feedburnerHostname>
<item>
    <title>Anti-inflammatory juice</title>
    <link>http://juicingtherainbow.com/2380/recipes/anti-inflammatory-juice/</link>
    <comments>
    http://juicingtherainbow.com/2380/recipes/anti-inflammatory-juice/#comments
    </comments>
    <pubDate>Fri, 14 Jun 2013 09:42:46 +0000</pubDate>
    <dc:creator>Andy Williams</dc:creator>
    <category><![CDATA[Recipes]]></category>
    <guid isPermaLink="false">http://juicingtherainbow.com/?p=2380</guid>
    <description><![CDATA[Inflammation is one of the main causes of disease, and a
    lot of the foods we eat contribute to the inflammation.  With chronic
    inflammation comes disease.  This juice is a powerful anti-inflammatory drink,
    and it's tasty too.]]></description>
    <wfw:commentRss>
    http://juicingtherainbow.com/2380/recipes/anti-inflammatory-juice/feed/
    </wfw:commentRss>
    <slash:comments>0</slash:comments>
</item>
<item>
    <title>Carrot pulp salad</title>
    <link>http://juicingtherainbow.com/2320/recipes/carrot-pulp-salad/</link>
    <comments>http://juicingtherainbow.com/2320/recipes/carrot-pulp-salad/#comments
```

Every post in the RSS feed has an entry like this.

RSS feeds provide an easy way for people to follow information they are interested in.

For example, if someone was interested in juicing, they could take the RSS feed from their favorite juicing websites and add them to an RSS reader, like Feedly.

Using a tool like Feedly, you can follow dozens of RSS feeds. RSS used this way allows you to scan hundreds of articles by title and description, and only click through to read the ones that you are really interested in.

That is why we have RSS feeds on our site.

WordPress has multiple RSS feeds

WordPress has a main RSS feed at **mydomain.com/feed**. Type that into your web browser substituting mydomain.com for your real domain name, and you'll see yours. However, WordPress also creates a lot of other RSS feeds.

For example, an RSS feed is created for each category of posts on your site. If you have a category called "roses", then there will be an RSS feed showing just the posts in the roses category.

To find the URL of any category page feed, simply go to the category page on the site and add **"feed"** to the end of it, like this:

```
← → C ⌂   ⓘ juicingtherainbow.com/category/disease/cancer/feed/

⠿ Apps  ⦿ My Current smartURL  ⚡ The Redmen TV - UN  ▦ KopTalk Members - p  ▯ ▯
```

```
<?xml version="1.0" encoding="UTF-8"?><rss version="2.0"
      xmlns:content="http://purl.org/rss/1.0/modules/content/
      xmlns:wfw="http://wellformedweb.org/CommentAPI/"
      xmlns:dc="http://purl.org/dc/elements/1.1/"
      xmlns:atom="http://www.w3.org/2005/Atom"
      xmlns:sy="http://purl.org/rss/1.0/modules/syndication/'
      xmlns:slash="http://purl.org/rss/1.0/modules/slash/"
      >

<channel>
      <title>Cancer &#8211; Juicing the Rainbow</title>
```

Other RSS feeds created by WordPress include RSS feeds for tag pages, author pages, comments, search results, and so on. You can read more about WordPress RSS feeds here if you're interested:

http://codex.WordPress.org/WordPress_Feeds

RSS feeds can help our pages get indexed

RSS feeds contain links to the pages on our website. We can use that fact to help our content get found more quickly by the search engines. To do this, we simply need to submit the RSS feed to an RSS directory, like Feedage.com.

Search Google for **RSS feed submission** and you'll find more sites where you can submit your main feed. I recommend only submitting it to 3 or 4 of the top RSS feed directories though.

When you post a new article on your site, the feeds on your site are updated, which in turn updates the feed on the RSS directories. These directories now contain a link back to your new article. The search engines monitor sites like this to find new content, so your new article is found very quickly.

Tasks to complete

1. Go and have a look at Feedly.com and signup for a free account. Subscribe to some feeds that are of interest and look through them to find articles that appeal to you. This will give you a good idea of how feeds can be helpful.

2. Since you currently have no posts on your site, you won't have any meaningful feeds. Once you have some published posts, go and find the various feed URLs (main feed, category feed, tag feed, author feed & search feed).

User Profile

When someone comes to your website, they often want to see who is behind the information. Your user profile in WordPress allows you to tell your visitors a little bit about yourself.

In the Dashboard, hover your mouseover **Users** in the navigation menu and then select **Your Profile**.

Your user profile will load.

At the top of the Profile screen you'll see a couple of settings:

Personal Options

Visual Editor	☐ Disable the visual editor when writing
Syntax Highlighting	☐ Disable syntax highlighting when editing code

Leave these both unchecked, as they disable useful features of the Dashboard. Under these options, you can change the color scheme of the Dashboard if you don't like the default.

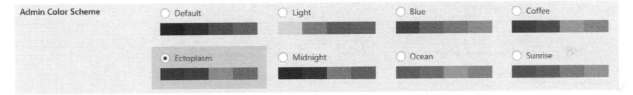

As you check an option, your Dashboard color scheme will change to reflect your choice. You may be spending a lot of time in your Dashboard, so choose a color scheme you like.

We then have these two options:

Keyboard Shortcuts	☐ Enable keyboard shortcuts for comment moderation. More information
Toolbar	☑ Show Toolbar when viewing site

I don't use keyboard shortcuts for comment moderation, but if you'd like to, enable the option and follow the "More Information" link to learn how to use it.

Show Toolbar when viewing site is an important option and should be checked. We will look at that later.

The next set of Profile options are for your name:

Name

Username	Andy
First Name	Andy
Last Name	Williams
Nickname *(required)*	Andy
Display name publicly as	Andy Williams ▾

Your username cannot be changed. It will be whatever you chose when you installed WordPress.

Enter your real first and last name (or your persona if you are working with a pen name).

Under nickname, you can write anything. I typically use my first name.

The **Display name publicly as** field is populated with names built from the personal information entered on this screen.

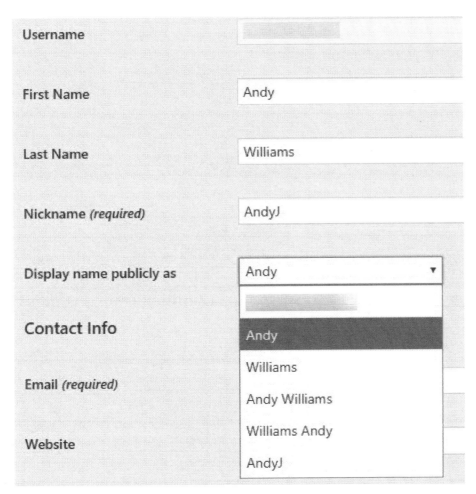

Whatever you choose will be the name used on each page of your website telling the visitors who wrote the article:

Hello world!

Welcome to WordPress. This is your first post. Edit or delete it, then start writing!

Andy

August 23, 2016

Edit

On the Twenty Sixteen theme, the name links to the author page, which shows all articles I have written on the site. Incidentally, that author page also has its own RSS feed (see earlier).

The next few options are for contact information.

The only one that is required here is the email address and we have talked earlier about how important that is. If you want to fill out the website field, you can, but this is more useful if you have multiple authors on your site, each with their own personal website.

Next in the profile is your **Biographical Info**.

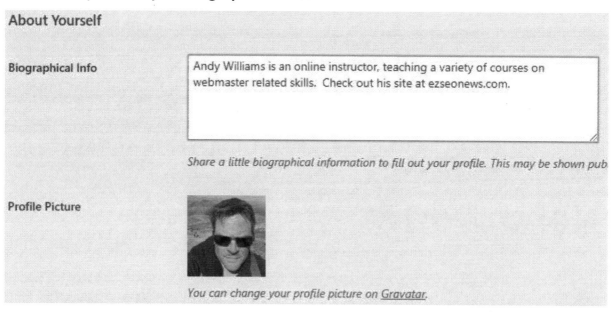

I recommend you fill in a short biography as some themes will show this on the author page. You can also see my profile picture in the screenshot. Chances are you won't have your photo there, as it needs to be set up on the Gravatar website. We'll look at that later in the book.

The author bio isn't displayed on the author page for the Twenty Sixteen theme, so here is a screenshot from my ezseonews.com website author page:

Andy Williams

About Andy Williams

Dr. Andy Williams is a Science teacher by training, but has now been working online for over a decade, specializing in search engine optimization and affiliate marketing. He publishes his free weekly Internet Marketing newsletter with tips, advice, tutorials, and more. You can subscribe to his free daily paper called the Google Daily and follow him on Facebook orTwitter. You can also follow me on Google +

EzSEO Newsletter #353 – Optimizing for Google's RankBrain

You can see my author bio which is pulled from the "Biographical Info" in the user profile. You can also see my photo (Gravatar).

My posts on the site are then listed below my bio.

Gravatars

A Gravatar is simply a photograph or image that you can connect to your email address.

Sites that use Gravatar information, like WordPress, will show that image whenever possible if you contribute something.

For example, your photo will show on your author page. It will also show on any WordPress site where you leave a comment (assuming you use that photo-linked email address when leaving the comment). Some themes can even show your photo after each post along with your author's bio. Here is the box that appears after every post of mine on the ezseonews.com website:

About Andy Williams

Dr. Andy Williams is a Science teacher by training, but has now been working online for over a decade, specializing in search engine optimization and affiliate marketing. He publishes his free weekly Internet Marketing newsletter with tips, advice, tutorials, and more. You can subscribe to his free daily paper called the Google Daily and follow him on Facebook orTwitter. You can also follow me on Google +

View all posts by Andy Williams →

OK, let's set up the Gravatar.

Go over to Gravatar.com and find the button or link to sign up.

You'll be asked to fill in your email address, a username, and a password.

Gravatar.com will send an email to your email address. You need to open it and click the confirmation link to activate your new Gravatar account.

On clicking that link, you'll be taken back to a confirmation page telling you that your WordPress.com account has been activated. You can then start using Gravatar by clicking the Sign in button.

When you log in you will then be taken to a screen that allows you to assign a photo to your email address:

Manage Gravatars

1. Pick email to modify

Add email address

Whoops, looks like you don't have any images yet! Add one by clicking here!
If you don't assign a Gravatar to your email address, a custom one will be dynamically generated fi settings of the website it appears on.

Just click the link and you'll be able to choose an image from a number of different places, including upload, from a URL, or from a webcam.

Once you've selected your image, you'll get an option to crop it.

You now need to rate your image (remember, we mentioned Gravatar ratings earlier when setting up WordPress):

Choose a rating for your Gravatar

Just click the appropriate button.

That's it. Your Gravatar should now be attached to your site's email address. Whenever you leave comments on a WordPress site, use that email address and your image will show up along with your comment (assuming they haven't turned Avatars off).

Tasks to complete

1. Go and claim your Gravatar.
2. Log in to your WordPress site and complete your user profile.
3. Find a WordPress site in your niche, and go leave a relevant comment. Watch as your image appears next to your comment.

Tools

The next main menu is called Tools, and it has three options:

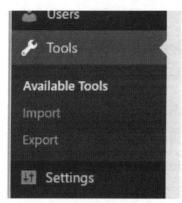

The **Available Tools** screen simply tells you how to convert your categories to tags, or vice versa.

Tools

Categories and Tags Converter

If you want to convert your categories to tags (or vice versa), use the Categories and Tags Converter available from the Import screen.

Clicking on the link will take you to the **Import** screen which has a link to a number of different tools, including the Categories and Tags Converter. If you want to use this or any other plugin on the import screen, I suggest you read the **Details** for the plugin by clicking the link under the plugin title.

The Tools menu also has an **Export** feature that allows you to export content from your site. It can then be imported into another site (using the previously mentioned **Import** screen). I have used this when I wanted to merge two or more websites into one larger website. Let's see the process.

To export content, click the **Export** menu:

Export

When you click the button below WordPress will crea

This format, which we call WordPress eXtended RSS (

Once you've saved the download file, you can use the

Choose what to export

(●) All content

This will contain all of your posts, pages, comments, c

( ) Posts

( ) Pages

( ) Media

Download Export File

You can choose to export all the site content, posts, pages, or media files.

If you select posts, you will be given more options including categories to export, export by author, date range or status (published, scheduled, draft, etc.).

Once you have made your selection, click the export button to download the export file to your computer.

To import the content into another website, install the relevant WordPress plugin on the Import screen:

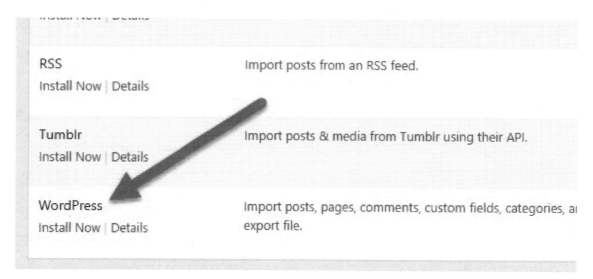

Click the **Install Now** link.

Once installed, the link under the plugin changes to **Run Importer**.

Click the **Run Importer** link and you'll see the following screen:

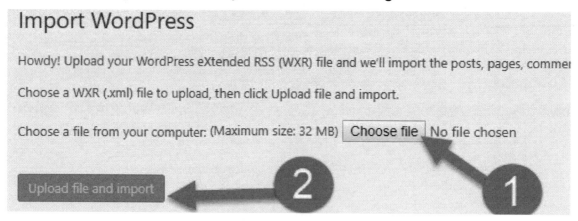

Choose the file and click **Upload file and import**.

Appearance menu

The **Appearance** menu contains these items:

This menu, as the name suggests, gives you access to settings that control the appearance of your site.

Clicking on the Appearance menu opens the themes setting page.

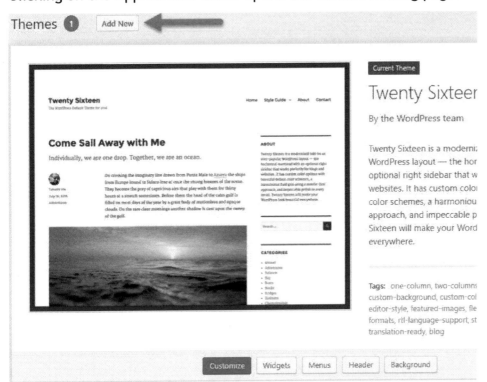

At the top of the themes screen, you have the option to **Add New** theme, which will search the WordPress theme repository for approved (and therefore generally safe) themes that you can install and use on your site.

NOTE: You will often hear people referring to WordPress themes as templates. While the two things are not totally the same thing, people often use the words interchangeably to mean the same.

If you have more than one theme installed, you'll see a thumbnail of each one. There will also be a search box at the top to help you search your installed themes.

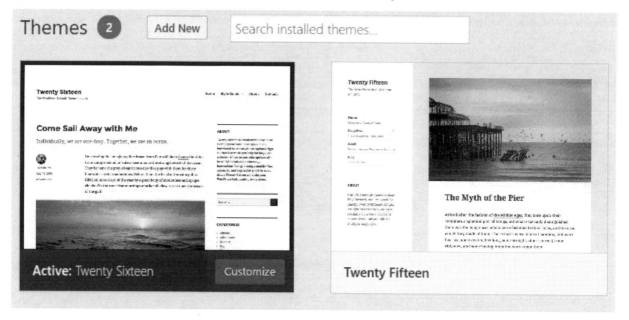

Your active theme is shown in the first position, with a **Customize** button next to the text **Active: Twenty Sixteen** (or whatever your active theme is called).

The customize button will take you to a live editor allowing you to make some design changes to the appearance of your site.

Click on the **Customize** button to open the editor:

74

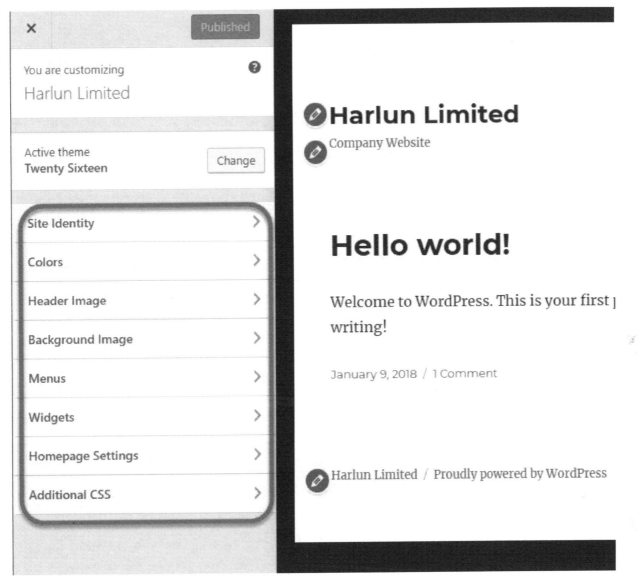

On the left is a menu that gives you access to site settings.

Most of these settings can also be found buried in the menus of the **Settings** sidebar menu. The advantage of editing them here is the live preview when you do make changes. You can see that live preview in the large window on the right.

At the top of the menu is Site Identity. If you click on that, you'll get access to these settings:

You can edit the site title and tagline and watch the preview display on the right update with the new settings.

There is an option to **Display Site Title and Tagline**. If you uncheck this, see what happens to the preview. The site title and tagline disappear. Try it.

Why might you want to remove the Site title and tagline?

Well, you might decide to use a header image/graphic instead so have no need for the text.

When you have finished playing around with the settings, click the arrow (<) in the top left to move back up one level in the menu system.

The next menu is the colors menu:

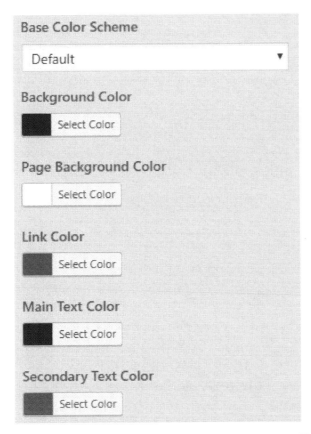

At the top, you'll see a drop-down box offering **Base Colour Schemes**.

Try the various color schemes and watch the preview panel.

Play around with the other color settings to see how they display on the preview screen. You can change colors by clicking the **Select Colour** button and then choosing from the palette.

If you go back up to the main menu again, **Header Image** is the next item in the list.

This allows you to upload a header image to be used across the top of every page on your site. If you do decide to use an image, make sure you turn off the Site Name and Tagline text (see earlier). Adding a header image is as easy as uploading it and cropping if necessary. Just be sure that the image you are trying to use is the correct size:

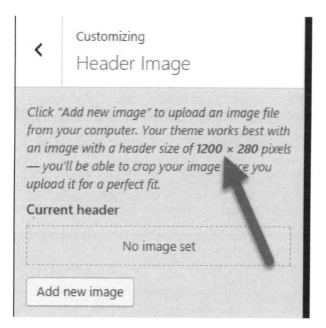

Customizing

Header Image

Click "Add new image" to upload an image file from your computer. Your theme works best with an image with a header size of **1200 × 280 pixels** — you'll be able to crop your image once you upload it for a perfect fit.

Current header

No image set

Add new image

The dimensions of the header image will vary between themes.

The next menu is the **Background Image** setting. This will place a background image on your page web pages. The image won't obscure the text, as the text is placed on a separate layer in the foreground.

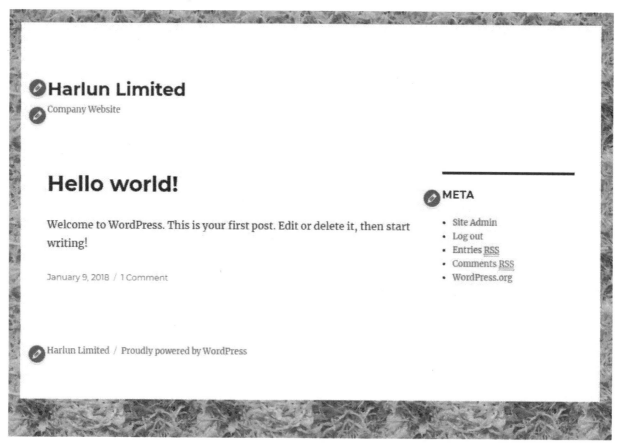

Harlun Limited
Company Website

Hello world!

Welcome to WordPress. This is your first post. Edit or delete it, then start writing!

January 9, 2018 / 1 Comment

META

- Site Admin
- Log out
- Entries RSS
- Comments RSS
- WordPress.org

Harlun Limited / Proudly powered by WordPress

There are a number of options displayed for these background images, but the available options will change depending on what you have selected in the **Preset** box:

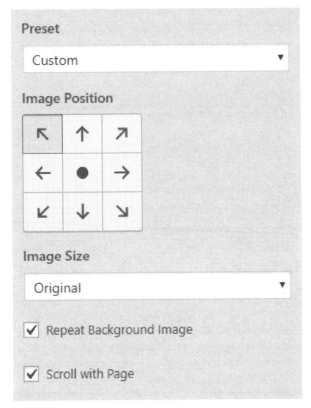

I'll leave you to explore these options yourself, as I don't recommend using a background image at all. A simple colored background is better in my opinion, as images often look messy and unprofessional.

I do recommend you upload an image and play around with the settings to see what they do. When you have finished, click the remove image to get rid of it.

The next item is the **Menus** settings. These allow you to select menus that you have created and use them on your website. We will look at this later.

Next up is the Widgets menu. Clicking that will open a screen showing you the widgetized areas of your theme. You can add/edit widgets on this screen, but I recommend you don't. The **Widget** screen in the Appearance menu is far easier to use as you will see later in this book.

If you have created a page on your site, then you will see the **Homepage Settings**.

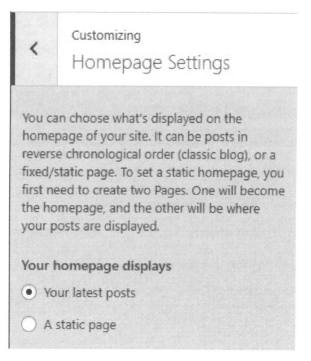

These options are identical to the ones we saw earlier in the **Reading Settings**.

NOTE: If you haven't created a WordPress PAGE, then you won't see this option here, or in the reading settings.

The final option in the **Customize** screen is **Additional CSS**. This is useful if you know CSS, as it allows you to override the defaults built into the theme. For example, if your theme does not underline links, you can add the CSS to force links to be underlined. However, CSS is beyond the scope of this book.

When you have finished playing with the customize settings, either save and publish your changes if you like the look of your site, or cancel to undo your experimentation.

For now, let's revisit themes.

Finding WordPress Themes, Installing and Selecting them

We had a brief look at installing themes earlier in the book, so we should know how to search for, and install, a new theme.

Click **Themes** under the **Appearance** menu.

Click the **Add New** button at the top of the themes screen.

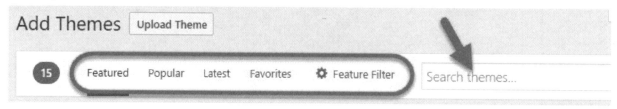

At the very top of this screen is a button, labeled "Upload Theme". If you bought or downloaded a theme from a website, it will come as a zip file. You can install it by clicking this button, selecting the file, and clicking Install.

There is a search box on this screen which is useful if you know the name of the theme you want to install.

There is also a menu at the top, with **Featured** selected by default. This will show you a list of the currently "featured" themes, which you can install.

Click on the **Popular** link to be offered a list of the most popular WordPress themes. This is often a good place to start since these are the themes that have been downloaded the most, or rated the highest.

If you want to see the latest WordPress themes to be accepted into the theme repository, click the **Latest** link.

The next item on the menu is **Favorites** but that will be empty if you haven't favorited any themes.

Finally, the **Feature Filter** gives you the chance to specify exactly what you are looking for.

| 15 | Featured | Popular | Latest | Favorites | ⚙ Feature Filter |

| Apply Filters |

Subject	Features	Layout
☐ Blog	☐ Accessibility Ready	☐ Grid Layout
☐ E-Commerce	☐ Custom Background	☐ One Column
☐ Education	☐ Custom Colors	☐ Two Columns
☐ Entertainment	☐ Custom Header	☐ Three Columns
☐ Food & Drink	☐ Custom Logo	☐ Four Columns
☐ Holiday	☐ Editor Style	☐ Left Sidebar
☐ News	☐ Featured Image Header	☐ Right Sidebar
☐ Photography	☐ Featured Images	

Make selections by checking the boxes and then click the **Apply Filters** button. WordPress will go away and find the themes that match the features you have selected.

You will see a list of thumbnails for all themes that match your filter criteria. You can mouseover each thumbnail to get more details of the theme, and to Install it.

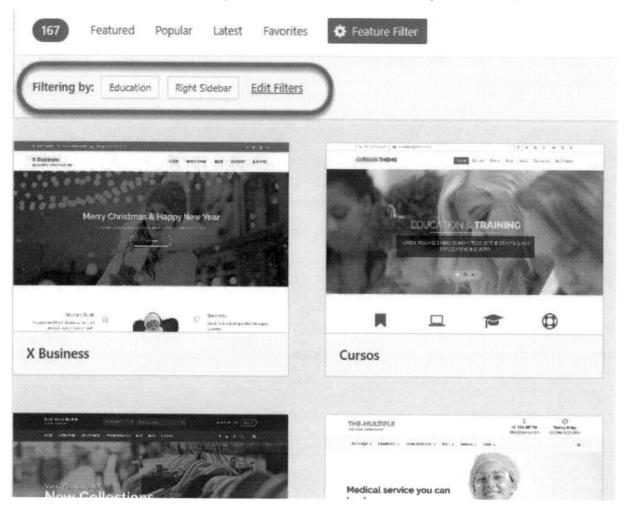

The preview button is well worth clicking before installing any new theme. A window opens to show you a preview of the theme, with headers, fonts, bullets etc., so you know exactly what your pages will look like.

If you like a theme, you can install it. If not, move onto the next one. Feel free to install a few themes. If you don't like them, you can always uninstall them easily enough.

When you install a theme, it will be added to your **Themes** page inside the **Appearance** menu. From there, you can activate it, or delete it if you decide not to use it.

If you mouseover an inactive theme, you'll see buttons to **Activate** or **Live Preview** the theme.

Live Preview allows you to see what the theme will look like on your site. The Live Preview opens with the same theme customize screen we saw earlier. If you want to activate one of the installed themes, simply click the **Activate** button.

The other option you have on this thumbnail is **Theme Details**. Clicking this will bring up more details about the theme, and a **Delete** link in case you want to delete it. How much more detail? Well, that depends on the author of the theme, and how much detail they included with the theme.

NOTE: As a matter of security, I recommend you uninstall any theme you are not using.

We are going to continue working with the Twenty Sixteen theme in this book, so I'll activate it and delete the other themes I installed.

Adding a custom graphic header to your site

Click **Header** in the **Appearance** menu.

There is a setting here that we need to explore. Essentially it allows you to upload your own graphic for the header of your website.

The only thing you need to get right is the width & height of the image you want to use. The dimensions differ depending on the theme. This screen will tell you what dimensions you need for your chosen theme.

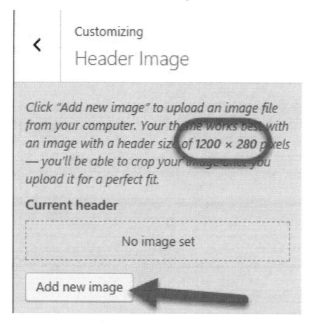

For the Twenty Sixteen theme, the image needs to be 1200 pixels wide and 280 pixels high. Any image that is not the correct size will look distorted on the site, so do stick to the suggested image dimensions.

Once you have created your image, click on the **Add New Image** button. You will be taken to a screen that has two tabs – **Media Library** and **Upload Files**.

The **Media Library** tab will show you all the images that you've uploaded to your site. Chances are it is currently blank.

Switch to the **Upload Files** tab, and you have a choice. You can drag and drop the image from your computer into the space around the button, or click the **Select Files** button and choose the file to upload from your computer.

Once the file has been uploaded, click on the **Select and Crop** button (bottom right).

You'll then be taken to a screen showing your header with a crop box around it. Resize and reposition the crop box so that your header is central, then click **Crop Image.**

The new logo image will be inserted into your site on the preview screen, so you can see how it looks. If it is OK, click the **Publish** button at the top.

To remove the header image, mouseover the **Previously uploaded** image and you'll get an "X" to remove it.

Remember that if you are using a logo image, you probably want to go back to the Site Identity section of the Customize screen and uncheck the **Display Site Title and Tagline**.

OK, close the **Customize** screen:

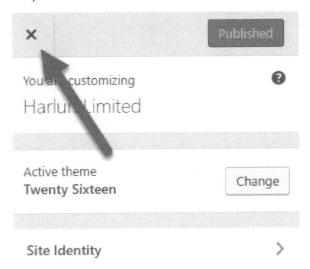

The theme Editor menu

The bottom item in the **Appearance** menu is the **Editor**. This allows you to edit the theme template files. This is an advanced topic requiring programming skills, so we won't be covering it here.

We've skipped over two of the Appearance menu items - **Widgets** and **Menus**. These are both very important, but they'll make a lot more sense once we have some posts published, so let's leave those until a little later on in the book.

Tasks to complete

1. Choose a theme you want to use. For your first site, I recommend you stick with Twenty Sixteen (you can always change it later), as we'll use it throughout this book as our reference theme.

2. Go to the Customize screen and try out the options.

3. Add a header graphic if you want to, but be sure to remove the Site Title and Tagline if you do.

Plugins

In this section, I want to explain what plugins are, where you can get them, and how to install them. I'll also walk you through the installation and configuration of a few important plugins.

In the Dashboard sidebar, you'll see the **Plugins** menu:

The "1" in a red circle means there is one plugin to update. See earlier in the book on how to update plugins, themes, and WordPress itself.

The menu has three options:

Installed Plugins – To view the current list of installed plugins.

Add New – To add a new plugin. You can also add a new plugin from the **Installed Plugin** screen.

Editor – This is a text editor that allows you to modify the code of the plugins. We won't be looking at this advanced topic.

Click on the installed plugins menu.

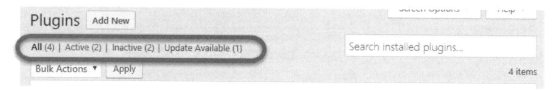

At the top of this screenshot is this:

All (4) | Active (2) | Inactive (2) | Update Available (1)

These groups refer to the plugins you have installed.

The number in brackets tell you how many plugins are in that group. We have a total of 4 plugins installed on this site, 2 are active, and one needs updating.

You may see something slightly different. For example, if you have deactivated a plugin that was once active, you might also see another group called **Recently Active**. You may also have a group called **Drop-ins** depending on the plugins you have installed. These are special types of plugins that alter core WordPress functionality.

To activate a plugin is easy. Just click the **Activate** link underneath the name of the plugin.

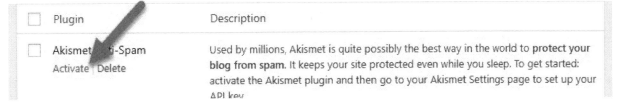

The menu at the top will change to reflect the newly activated plugin.

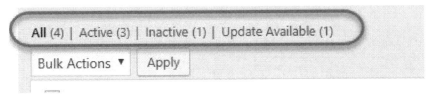

Deactivating is just as easy. The **Deactivate** link is present for all active plugins.

We can view just the active plugins, or just the inactive plugins, by clicking those links at the top:

NOTE: It is not a good idea to keep inactive plugins installed. If you do not need a plugin, deactivate and delete.

For security reasons, whenever you see the **Update Available** group, go in and update the plugin(s). Click the update available link to see which plugins have updates pending.

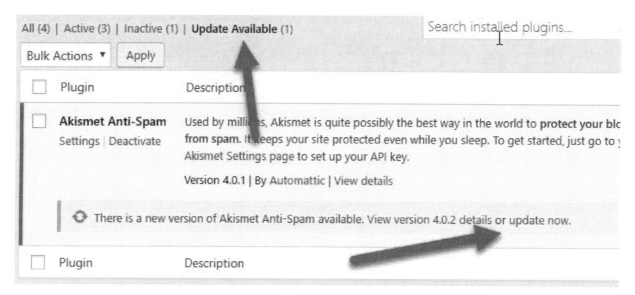

Once updated, the **Update Available** link at the top will disappear.

As you saw earlier, you can also handle all updates by using the Dashboard's **Updates** menu.

I don't want to use Akismet or Hello Dolly (these were pre-installed with WordPress), so let's delete them now.

NOTE: Akismet is a good anti-spam plugin but it went commercial a while back, meaning it's no longer free for commercial websites. If your site is non-profit, feel free to activate Akismet.

Deleting plugins

To delete a plugin, it needs to be inactive. If you have an active plugin you want to delete, first deactivate it.

To delete a plugin, click the **Delete** link under the plugin name (the delete link only appears on inactive plugins):

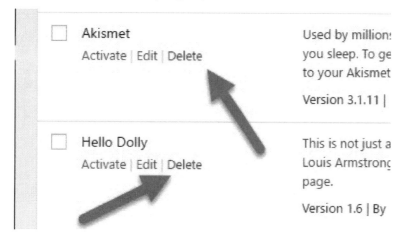

You will be asked to confirm the deletion, so click OK. The plugin and all its files will be removed from your server.

If you have more than one plugin to delete, there is a quicker way to remove multiple plugins in one go:

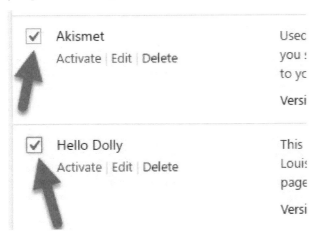

Just check the box next to each plugin you want to delete, then, in the **Bulk Actions** drop-down box at the bottom, select **Delete**.

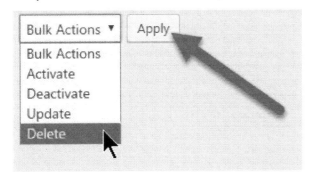

Click the Apply button to carry out the deletion. You will get a confirmation screen like the one we saw a moment ago, asking you to confirm that you really do want to delete all selected plugins.

NOTE: The bulk action drop-down box also allows you to activate, deactivate, and update multiple plugins in one go.

Plugin-injected menu items

Some plugins may add their own menu items, like this one:

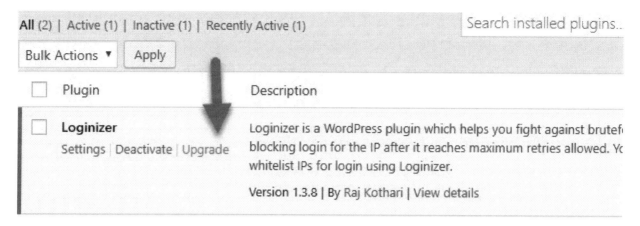

This upgrade link takes you to a website to buy an upgraded version of the plugin. Don't let that confuse you with the updating of plugins we saw earlier. Since plugins (and themes) are created by third-party programmers, this type of extra menu item is quite common.

Installing important plugins

Before we look at the plugins, I need to let you know that plugins are updated frequently, and their appearance may change a little. However, these changes are usually minor cosmetic changes, so if you don't see exactly what I am showing you in these screenshots, look around. The options will be there somewhere.

Let's go ahead and install a few very important plugins, then configure them.

UpdraftPlus

Backing up anything on a computer should be a priority. While good web hosts do keep backups for you, if your site gets infected with any kind of malicious code and you don't find out about it for a while, all their backups could be infected.

I always recommend you have your own backup plan, and fortunately, there is a great plugin that can help.

Click the **Add New** item in the **Plugins** menu.

Search for Updraft.

Find, install, and activate, this plugin:

You'll have a new **UpdraftPlus Backups** section in the settings menu. Click on it to access the settings of this plugin.

You can take manual backups on the **Current Status** tab:

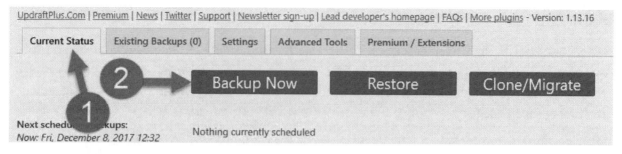

More powerful still is the ability to schedule automatic backups of your site. To do that, click on the **Settings** tab.

Choose a frequency and the number of backups to retain.

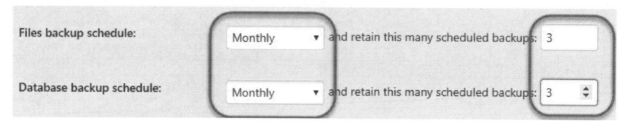

Now scroll down and click **Save Changes** at the bottom.

You will notice that on this screen, you also have the option of using remote storage for your backups. If you have a Dropbox account, that is a great place to send backups. They'll be off your server, and safe if you ever need them. You can also get backups emailed to you, though full backups can be very large.

I won't go into details on setting this up, just follow the instructions that are included with the plugin.

Contact Form 7

It's important that site visitors can contact you, so let's install the best-known contact form plugin. It's called Contact Form 7.

Install and activate the plugin.

This will add a new menu called Contact in the sidebar of the Dashboard.

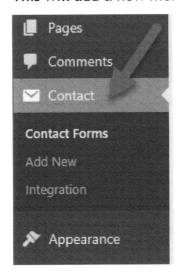

If you click on **Contact Forms**, you can see that the plugin created one for you.

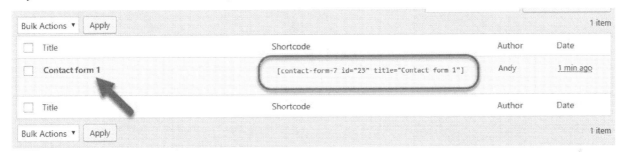

We will use this one, as it is a perfectly good contact form. You just need to copy the **Shortcode**.

Create a new page by clicking on **Add New** in the **Pages** menu.

Add a title for the page, e.g. Contact Form, Contact, or Contact Us.

Paste the shortcode into the editor:

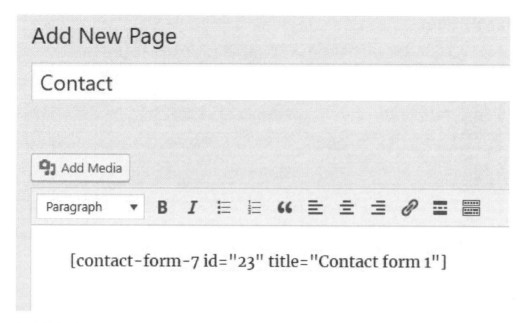

Add New Page

Contact

Add Media

Paragraph ▾ B *I* ☰ ☰ " ☰ ☰ ☰ 🔗 ☰ ☰

[contact-form-7 id="23" title="Contact form 1"]

Publish the page.

You can now visit the page by clicking on the permalink:

Edit Page Add New

Page published. View page

Contact

Permalink: http://harlun.co.uk/contact/ Edit

When the page opens, you will see the contact form.

Auto Terms of Service and Privacy Policy

This plugin adds a privacy policy and terms of service document to your site. I call these pages (together with the contact form) the "legal pages" because they are essential for all websites.

Go to **Add New** plugin and search for **auto terms.**

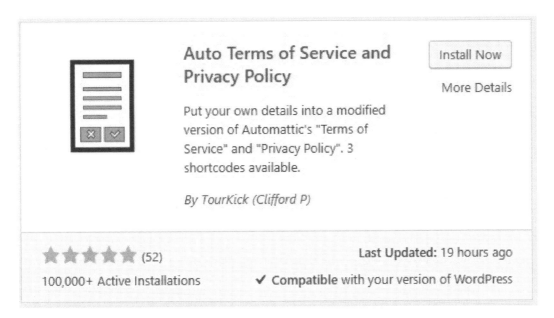

Install and activate the plugin.

This plugin installs a menu inside the main **Settings** menu.

Click on **Auto TOS & PP**.

There may be a splash screen asking to share data with them, but you can skip that if you want. Once through that screen, there is a form you need to fill. It's fairly intuitive, so go ahead and fill it in.

Once you've filled that, change the top **On/Off** switch to **On / Displaying**:

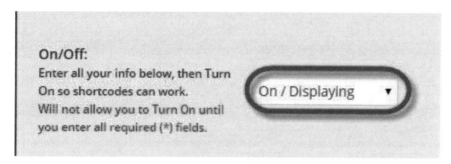

Click on the **Save** button at the bottom.

If you have missed any required fields, the on/off switch won't change to **On / Displaying**, so check your form if you have issues.

We need to create some pages to hold the documents, but don't close this screen as we'll need these "shortcodes":

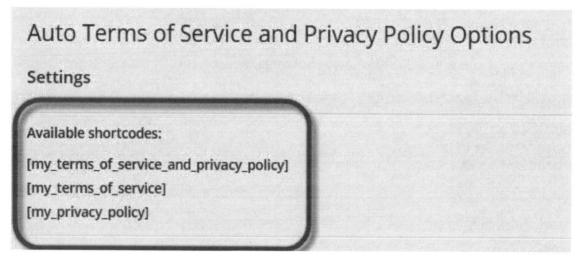

Under the **Pages** menu in the sidebar, right-click **Add New** and select to open in a new tab.

Enter the title "Privacy Policy".

In the WYSIWYG editor, paste in the shortcode for the privacy policy:

Now click the **Publish** button on the right.

Once the page is published, open the page in your browser (using the permalink) to see your new Privacy Policy.

Repeat this process, adding a page for the Terms of Service (page title "Terms").

OK; you now have a Privacy Policy and Terms of Service page created. If you need a disclaimer, you'll need to manually create that. Just create a WordPress Page, and add the disclaimer to the WYSIWYG editor. If you need help with your disclaimer, search Google for "sample disclaimer". Depending on the type of site you run, you might need a medical disclaimer, outbound links disclaimer, etc.

Yoast SEO

Go to **Add New** plugin and search for **Yoast SEO**.

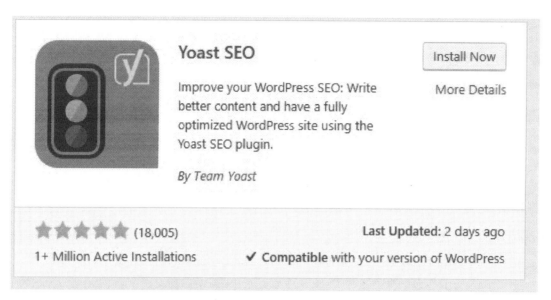

Install and activate the plugin.

This plugin installs a new menu in the sidebar called **SEO**.

Click on **Dashboard** in the **SEO** menu to get to the **General** Yoast SEO settings.

Across the top, you'll see some tabs. Click on the **Features** tab and enable the **Advanced Settings Pages**:

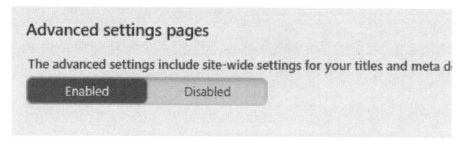

Scroll to the bottom and save changes. Your SEO menu in the sidebar will now have a lot more options!

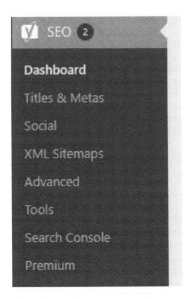

We'll only look at the essential ones.

The first item in the menu is **Dashboard** which we have already been introduced to. If you click on that, the plugin takes you to the general settings, Dashboard tab. This tab will tell you if there are any problems or improvements that can be made to your site.

Across the top, you see other tabs – **General, Features, Your Info, Webmaster Tools** and **Security.**

The **General** tab offers you help, even giving you a video tour of the plugin. It is well worth watching.

Under the video is the configuration wizard. Again, this is something you can go through if you want. If you make a mess of things, just come back to the General tab and click the **Restore Default Settings** button. It's there if you need it.

We have briefly seen the **Features** tab when we enabled the advanced settings pages earlier. This tab allows you to turn features on or off. Apart from the setting we have already changed, I recommend you leave the other features as they are.

On the **Your Info** tab, you can specify if your site relates to a company or person. I recommend you do that now.

We'll ignore the **Webmaster Tools** tab.

On the **Security** tab, enable the **Advanced part of the Yoast SEO meta box.** This is useful if you want to make changes to the "visibility" of a post or page.

The next item in the SEO menu is **Titles & Metas.** Click on it.

There are a number of tabs across the top.

The General tab lets you change the separator symbol to be used in titles. For example, you might want to include the title of a post and the company name in your web page titles. It might look like this:

Are Memory Foam Mattresses Really Superior? - Sweet Dreams Limited

See the separator between the title and the company name? That is the title separator. Choose whichever one you want.

Under the title separator, you have a couple of "SEO" options enabled. With modern day SEO, I personally don't use these so disable them. Before you do, go and look at **All Posts** in the **Posts** menu. Look at the table column headers. You'll see SEO and Readability. These two are added by those settings in the Yoast SEO screen. Once disabled, these two columns disappear.

The homepage, posts types, taxonomies and archives tabs define how the title and meta description are created when the web page loads. There are some other options on some of these tabs as well, which we will look at shortly.

On the Homepage tab, what you see will depend on how you have your homepage setup. If you are using a static page for your homepage, there isn't much to see on this tab. All homepage settings will be defined on the edit page screen for that page. You'd edit the title and meta description directly on the page edit screen.

However, if you have your site set up to show posts on the homepage (the default), you will see boxes where you can enter title and meta description "templates".

The template is simply a set of variables which will be replaced at the time the page is rendered. Currently, the homepage title template looks like this:

Homepage

Title template:	%%sitename%% %%page%% %%sep%% %%sitedesc%%
Meta description template:	

The variables all start and end with %%.

The first variable in that template is %%sitename%%. This will be replaced by the site's name when the page is rendered.

The homepage of a WordPress site showing blog posts on the homepage will be broken up into multiple pages (paginated). By default, the main homepage will show the last 10 posts, then a second page will be created to hold the next 10, and so on. These "homepages" will all be linked to one another. The %%page%% variable inserts the page number with context (e.g. page 1 of 3).

We then have the %%sep%% variable which will insert the separator character we looked at earlier.

Finally, the title template uses %%sitedesc%% which inserts the site's tagline.

As you can see, the Meta Description can also be set up to use variables. You can find a full list of available variables if you click the **Help Center** link which you'll find just under the tabs. That help has two sections you should check out – **Basic Variables** and **Advanced Variables**.

I would recommend you leave the default templates settings for the homepage.

On the **Post Types** tab, you can see the now familiar template boxes for title and description of posts, pages & media on your site. Again, I would leave these default settings for title templates, but for meta description templates, I personally use %%excerpt%%. The excerpt is a description that you can add to every post and page you create within WordPress. We will see how to add excerpts to posts and pages later in the book. The excerpt is a natural match for the meta description of your page.

Add **%%excerpt%%** to each description template on the Post Types tab.

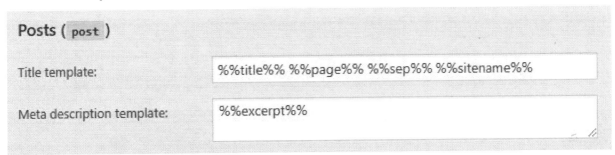

If a post or page on your site does not have an excerpt, then this variable will automatically generate one from the content on the page.

The other options you have for the three post types (posts, pages, and media) are shown below:

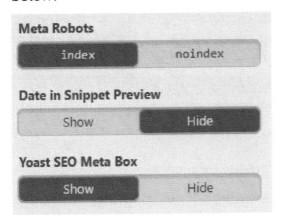

The **Meta Robots** setting here is the global setting, which can be over-ridden on a post by post basis (which is why we enabled that setting on the security tab a minute ago). This setting will determine whether the content is indexed by the search engines. Obviously, you want your posts in the search engines, so this should be left as **index**.

Pages are a little different to posts, especially the way I use them. We'll discuss these differences later, but just so you know, I often set the meta robots of my pages to noindex.

The second option is the **Date** in **Snippet Preview.**

If you are creating a website where the date of the post is important, then you can select to show the date in the snippet preview. I personally don't create sites where the date is important, so I leave this to hide.

The final option is the Yoast SEO Meta Box. When you add a new post or page, you'll see the Yoast SEO Meta box on the edit screen:

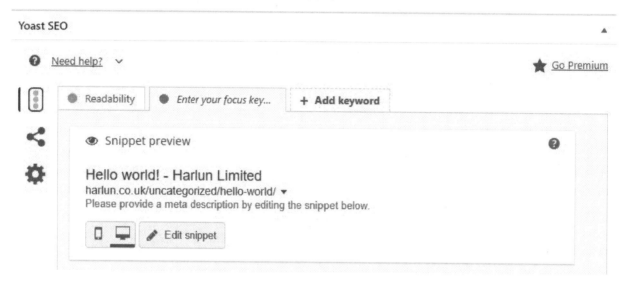

This Meta box gives us a lot of power, including the ability to override the default settings that we are currently looking at.

e.g. We have post types set to "index" in the general settings, but if we wanted to override that and create a post that we didn't want to be indexed, we could set the noindex from within Yoast meta box just for that one post.

We, therefore, want to keep the Yoast meta box visible for all post types.

OK, if you have made any changes to the Post Types settings, save changes and let's look at the taxonomies tab.

The important settings on this screen are for the category and tag pages.

We haven't looked at categories or tags yet, so this may be a little confusing. For now, just leave the default title settings. There is a new variable being used in the default template, so check out the Help Center to see what the variable does.

In the Categories meta description template, add the **%%category_description%%** variable. This will insert the category description as the meta description when the page is loaded in a browser.

In the Tags meta description template, add the **%%tag_description%%** variable. This will insert the tag description as the meta description when the page is loaded in a browser.

Save your changes.

Click on the **Archives** tab. This tab contains settings for some "archive" pages, namely author and date archives plus some special pages (search & 404).

The problem with archive pages like author and date is that they can cause duplicate content in the search engines. Search engines hate duplicate content and can penalize your site for it.

What I recommend you do is set the Meta Robots to **noindex** in both cases. You'll see the **Date Archive** is set to noindex by default, so just change the author archives setting. You won't be losing anything by deactivating the archives. All posts will still be found in the category and tag pages, and via your on-site navigation system.

Make sure you save your changes.

Before moving on, do go through the variables that have been used in these title templates. See what each variable does, so you can work out how the titles will look when a page is loaded in a web browser.

The final tab in the Title & Metas settings is the **Other** tab. This defines some sitewide settings.

The only option I am going to change is to set the **Subpages of archives** to **noindex**. This again is just to help prevent duplicate content showing up in the search engines.

OK, so that is titles & metas set up.

The next menu in the SEO settings is for **Social** integration. Click on that.

We are going to go through this quite quickly.

On the **Accounts** tab, you can enter your social media URLs. These social profiles relate to the site, not to you personally. If you have a Facebook page for your website, then add the URL here. The same applies to all the other social profiles - only add them if they are profiles specific to your website.

On the **Facebook** tab, you have some interesting options. The **open graph meta data** should be left enabled. This basically defines what information is shared when someone shares your post on social media. It's not just Facebook that uses open graph data, which is why we want to leave it enabled.

If you have ever shared anything on Facebook, you'll know that quite often there is an image attached to the post you are sharing. That image is taken from the web page you are sharing. With the settings on this screen, you can define a default image that will be used if there are no images within the post on your site. This is actually a good idea. You can create a small square or rectangular "logo" that will become the fallback image when someone shares a piece of your content that does not have an image.

I'm not going to go through any more of the social settings with this plugin. If you want to learn more, check out the help center which will show you a video related to the options you are currently exploring.

On the **XML Sitemap page**, make sure the sitemap functionality is enabled (it is by default). This will create a sitemap for you and automatically update it whenever new content is added to the site.

Before the sitemap can work, you need to save **Permalinks**. If you didn't do that earlier, do it now. You can find permalinks under the **Settings** menu. Just go to the permalinks screen, scroll to the bottom and click **Save Changes**. Your sitemap should now load.

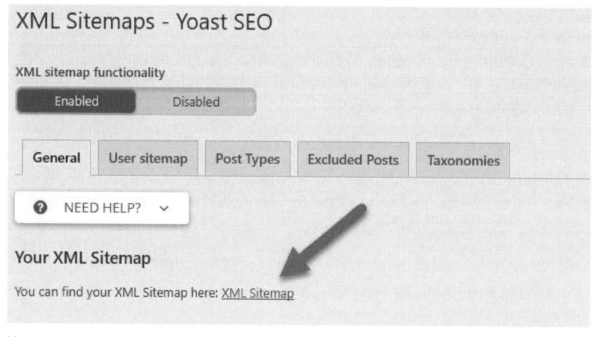

Here is my sitemap at the moment:

XML Sitemap

Generated by **YoastSEO**, this is an XML Sitemap, meant for consumption by search engines.

You can find more information about XML sitemaps on **sitemaps.org**.

This XML Sitemap Index file contains 3 sitemaps.

Sitemap	Last Modified
http://harlun.co.uk/post-sitemap.xml	2018-01-11 10:52 +00:00
http://harlun.co.uk/page-sitemap.xml	2018-01-11 11:09 +00:00
http://harlun.co.uk/category-sitemap.xml	2018-01-11 10:52 +00:00

You can see that there are three entries. Each of these link to another sitemap. The top one is a sitemap containing the posts on the site, the second is a sitemap of the pages on the site and the third is a sitemap of category pages on the site.

The **XML Sitemaps** settings in Yoast SEO control what will be added to the sitemap.

For example, on the **User Sitemap** tab, the author sitemap is disabled. If you enable it, the main sitemap will then include an author sitemap. Since the goal of a sitemap is to get important posts indexed, the author sitemap is not necessary. Important posts will already be in the posts sitemap.

If you click on the **Post Types** tab, you can see that you can exclude posts, pages or media from the sitemap. Media is not in the sitemap by default, whereas posts and pages are. This makes sense for most websites, as we want posts and pages to be found by the search engines.

The **Exclude Posts** tab allows you to exclude posts or pages on a one-by-one basis. All posts and pages have an ID. It's simply a number. If you add the post ID to this box, it will be excluded from the sitemap.

The easiest way to find a post ID is to go to the **All Posts** screen (or **All Pages**) and move your mouseover the post/page title. Your browser will display the post URL in the bottom left:

harlun.co.uk/wp-admin/post.php?post=1&action=edit

The post ID is the number after **?post=**

In this case, the postID is 1.

Finally, on the **Taxonomies** tab, you can turn on/off category & tag page sitemaps. These are in the sitemap by default, and you can leave those default settings.

Make sure you save changes.

You can view your sitemap by clicking the **XML Sitemap** button at the top of the General sitemap settings page. The sitemap will open in a new window.

We'll be looking at other SEO settings on a post by post (and page by page) basis as we go through the book, but for now, we can move on.

WordPress Security

I would recommend you check out a free plugin called All in One WP Security.

It is a great way to secure your WordPress website from hackers. I'll warn you that the plugin is quite complicated and can lock you out of the Dashboard if you set it up too aggressively. I, therefore, won't be covering it in this book. I simply don't want readers to face problems and then have no one to ask for help.

If you want to see a video tutorial I created for setting up this plugin, you can watch it here:

https://ezseonews.com/secureit

If you want a more comprehensive look at WordPress Security, including a more detailed set of tutorials for this plugin, I have a course called "WordPress Security – How To Stop Hackers" on Udemy. There is a generous discount available to readers via this link:

http://ezseonews.com/udemy

Note, that page lists all my courses. Just look for the WordPress Security course if that is the one that interests you.

Tasks to complete

1. Delete any pre-installed plugins.
2. Install Updraft Plus and set it up.

3. Create a contact form using Contact Form 7.
4. Install Auto Terms of Service and Privacy Policy and create the "legal" pages.
5. Install Yoast SEO and configure it.
6. Set up your sitemap.

Comments

I mentioned earlier that a lot of people turn comments off because they can't be bothered with comment moderation. The way I see it, comments are the life and soul of a website and help to keep visitors engaged with you and your content. You need to offer visitors this chance to connect with you. Therefore, you really should keep comments turned on.

We have already configured the "discussion" settings to blacklist comments with known spam content (using the blacklist you found by searching on Google), and that will cut down on comment spam considerably. However, there are dedicated anti-spam plugins available as well.

If you are running a non-commercial website, I recommend you use Akismet. It is probably the best anti-spam plugin available. It is for non-commercial use only though, and commercial sites need to pay for it.

I am reluctant to recommend a free comment spam plugin because most of the ones I have tried did not work effectively. The All-In-One Security plugin I recommended earlier in the book does include some great anti-spam features, so do investigate those. You will find them in the **Spam Prevention** menu within the main menu of the plugin.

I personally use a plugin called WP-SpamShield. It is excellent, but it is not free. Search Google if you want to look at that one.

Moderating comments

When people comment, their comments won't go live until you approve them. This is how we set the site up earlier. If you had comments set on auto-approve, you'd most likely find so many spam comments on your site that you'd be pulling your hair out. Manual approval is the only way to go, and it does not have to take a long time.

Let's see how easy it is to moderate comments.

If you click on **Comments** in the sidebar, you are taken to the comments section.

Across the top is a menu with All, Pending, Approved, Spam, Trash:

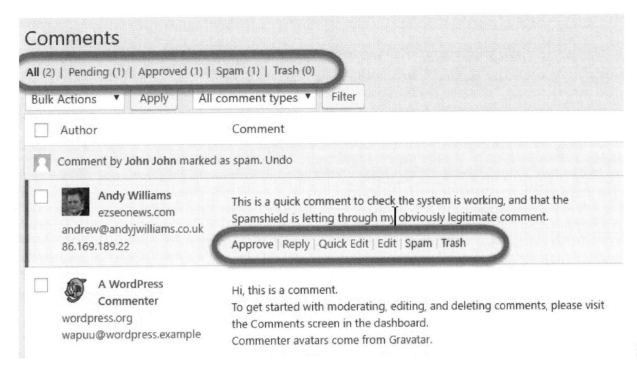

Comments

All (2) | Pending (1) | Approved (1) | Spam (1) | Trash (0)

Bulk Actions ▼   Apply   All comment types ▼   Filter

☐   Author   Comment

▨   Comment by **John John** marked as spam. Undo

☐   [avatar] **Andy Williams**   This is a quick comment to check the system is working, and that the
         ezseonews.com   Spamshield is letting through my obviously legitimate comment.
         andrew@andyjwilliams.co.uk
         86.169.189.22   Approve | Reply | Quick Edit | Edit | Spam | Trash

☐   [avatar] **A WordPress**   Hi, this is a comment.
         Commenter   To get started with moderating, editing, and deleting comments, please visit
         wordpress.org   the Comments screen in the dashboard.
         wapuu@wordpress.example Commenter avatars come from Gravatar.

Lower down you can see a comment I added to my site. When I added the comment, I used an email address linked to a Gravatar. That's why my photo is there. When you leave a comment on a WordPress site, your photo will show up too if you use a Gravatar-linked email address.

If you hover your mouseover a comment in the list, a menu appears underneath that comment, which you can click to Approve, Reply, Quick Edit, Edit, send to Spam or send to Trash.

If the comment is OK, click the Approve link. If the comment is clearly not spam, but you don't want to approve it, then click on **Trash**. If the comment is spam, click the spam link.

NOTE: Remember the **WP All-In-One Security** plugin? It has a nice feature that will automatically block comments from the IP addresses of comments in the spam folder. You'll find that by using this feature, you can improve spam recognition, and make your job of moderation easier.

You can also edit comments if you want to remove something (like a link) or correct a spelling error from an otherwise good comment.

I recommend you don't reply to comments until you approve them. My typical workflow is this:

1. Moderate comments.
2. Go to the Approved comments by clicking the Approved link at the top.
3. Reply to comments that need a reply.

4. Go to the **Trash** folder and empty it.

In the screenshot above, you will see a (1) next to the spam link. Click on the spam link to see what the spam folder contains.

You can see the comment and author for each comment in the list. If you decide that a comment is not spam, mouseover it and click **Not Spam** from the menu. The comment will be sent to the **Pending** pile and await moderation.

You also have the option to **Delete Permanently**. To delete all spam in the spam folder, you can simply click the **Empty Spam** button at the bottom. When you do delete spam, it is permanently removed.

The **Trash** folder holds all comments that were sent to the trash. Like the Spam folder, you can retrieve comments that are in the trash (if you need to) using the mouseover menu.

Finally, we have the **Approved** list. These are all comments on your site that have been approved. Click the link in the menu at the top to view them.

All comments in the Approved list have a mouseover menu as well, allowing you to **Reply** to the comment if you want to. You can, of course, change your mind about an "approved comment", and send it to spam or trash if you want to, or even **Unapprove** it if you want to think about it.

What kinds of Comments should you send to Spam/Trash?

You will get a lot of comments that say things like "nice blog", or "Great job". I suggest you trash all comments like this because they are spam comments. Their only purpose is to try and get a backlink from your site to theirs, through flattery.

I recommend you only approve comments that:

1. Add something to the main article, either with more information, opinions or constructive information. That means never approving a comment that could have been written without that person ever reading your post. Comments MUST add something to

your content. If they don't I suggest you send them to the Trash.

2. Never approve a comment where the person has used a keyword phrase for their name. You'll see people using things like "best Viagra online", or "buy XYZ online" as their name. No matter how good the comment is, trash it. What many spammers do is copy a paragraph from a good webpage on another website, and use that as their comment. The comment looks great, but the name gives away the fact that the comment is spam.

3. I would suggest you never approve trackbacks or pingbacks. Most will not be real anyway.

With comments, be vigilant and don't allow poor comments onto your site as they will reflect badly on both you and your website.

Here are three spammy comments left on one of my websites. All three would go straight to spam without hesitation:

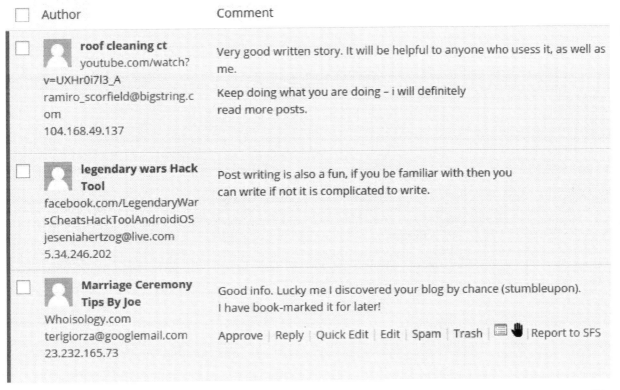

These comments are totally irrelevant to the content they are commenting on. You'll get a lot of comments like this. Spammers seem to think that a bit of flattery is all that is required to get a comment approved.

Also, check out the names of the "people" leaving each comment.

Tasks to complete

1. Install an anti-spam plugin if you want to use one, or look into the anti-spam

features of the All-In-One Security plugin and enable those.

2. Whenever there are comments on your site, moderate them. Spam or Trash any comments that are not "adding to the conversation".

Media Library

Media includes things like images and video that you want to use in posts, as well as other downloads you want to offer your visitors, e.g. PDF files.

The media library is a convenient storage area for all such items.

You can go and have a look at your Media Library by clicking on **Library** in the **Media** menu. All items are shown as a thumbnail. Clicking on a thumbnail will open the **Attachment Details** screen, which shows you the media item, URL, Title, etc. You even have some basic editing features if you need to crop, scale or rotate an image.

Uploading stuff to your media library is really very easy.

You will usually add media directly from the **Add Post** screen when typing a piece of content. However, if for example, you have a lot of images that you want to upload at any one time, it is often quicker to do it directly in the Media library.

How to Upload New Media

Click on **Add New** in the **Media** menu, or, on the **Media Library** page, click the **Add New** button at the top.

Uploading media is as simple as dragging and dropping where it says "Drop files here":

(You can also click the **Select Files** button and select them directly from your hard disk.)

To drag and drop something, open the file manager on your computer. Select the file(s) you want to upload and click and hold the left mouse button on the selected items. Now move your mouse, dragging the items to the dashed box in the Media Library screen. You can then release the mouse button, dropping those files into the Media

Library.

Upload New Media

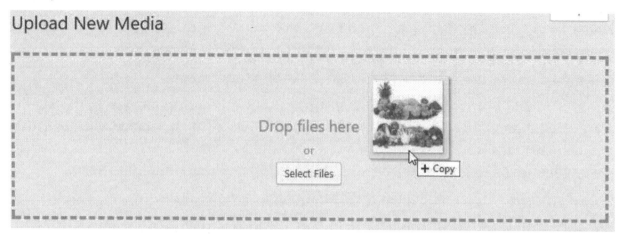

You can see I have dragged an image over the box. When I drop it there, the image is uploaded to my library. When the upload is complete, you'll be shown a thumbnail of the image:

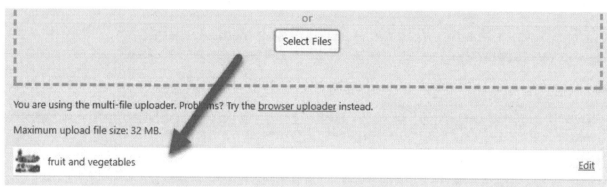

Clicking the edit link to the right of this thumbnail to open the **Edit Media** screen. This screen allows you to add a caption, ALT text, and description, for the media page that is created for your image. To access the actual media page created, click the permalink at the top of this screen:

You'll be taken to a web page that has been created by WordPress, just for the image. You'll see that the post has a comment section at the end. Yes, it is a real live webpage.

Have a look at the URL of that post. The URL will use the filename of the image to construct the web page's filename.

Chances are you won't actually use this page on your site unless you run some kind of image/photo site. However, know that it's there.

Click on **Library** in the **Media** menu.

You should see your uploaded image:

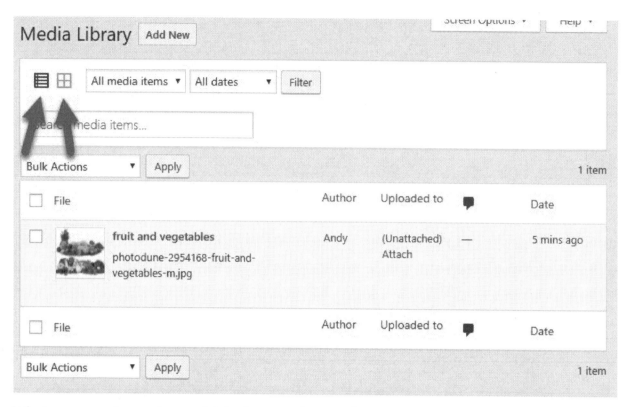

What you see depends on which view you have selected. See those two icons top left? Click on each one to see what they do.

In the screenshot above, you can see that the image I uploaded is not "attached". That means it is not being used on any post or page. We will look at how to add an image (or video) to a post later in this book. But for now, just try uploading a few images to get the hang of things.

NOTE: There are some file formats that WordPress will not let you upload for security reasons. PHP files are one example. If you want to upload a file so that you can offer it as a download on your site, but it is not accepted for upload, then zip it up and upload the zipped file instead.

At the top of the media library screen, you'll see some filtering options:

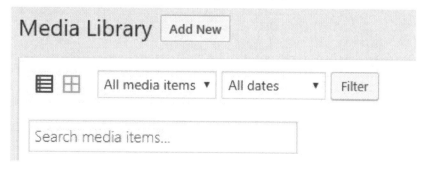

The two drop-down boxes allow you to view only a specific type of media, e.g. images,

116

or only those media items that were uploaded in a particular month.

We've already looked at the first two buttons that change the view of your uploaded media. Select that first button to show the table view.

Each item has the now familiar mouse-over menu which allows you to **Edit, Delete Permanently,** or **View,** that media item.

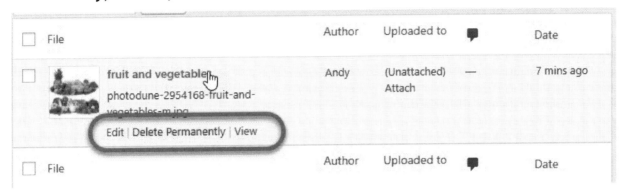

There is a column showing you the date the item was added to your library. In my screenshot, it says 7 minutes ago.

Note that columns in the media library are sortable by clicking the title of the column.

Mouseover a column header to see an "ascending/descending" arrow:

Just click the header to re-order.

If you have uploaded more images, try clicking the column headers to order your images by each column.

If there are columns you don't use and don't want to see, you can hide them by using the screen options. Remember those?

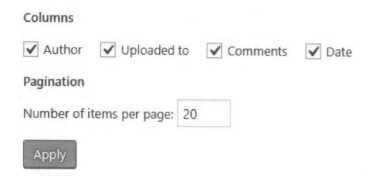

Columns

☑ Author   ☑ Uploaded to   ☑ Comments   ☑ Date

Pagination

Number of items per page: 20

Apply

Just unclick whichever items you don't want to see. You can even specify how many media items you see per page in your library.

If you have a lot of media in your library, there is a handy search feature:

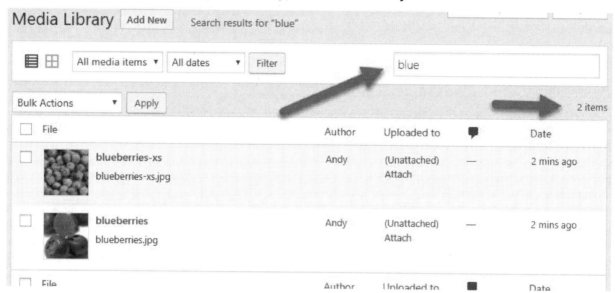

In the screenshot above, I searched for blue. The results returned the two media items including the word "blue". The search feature will look for your search text in both the title of the media and its description. If the word appears in either, it is shown in the search results.

To cancel the search filter, click on the "X" in the search box:

.. and press enter to refresh the results.

The media library also gives you **Bulk Actions** (something that can be applied to multiple items in one go).

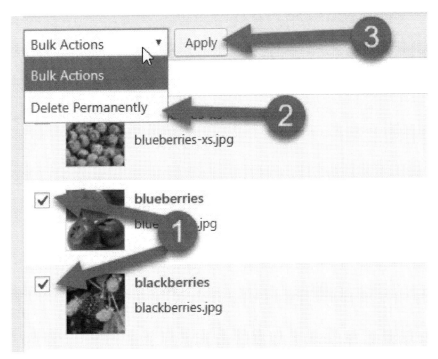

Next to each media item is a checkbox. If you want to delete several media items, you can check each one, and then select **Delete Permanently** from the **Bulk Actions** drop-down box. Click **Apply** to delete the checked items.

That's it for the Media Library for now. We will come back to this when we look at how to add content to your site using the What You See Is What You Get (WYSIWYG), document editor later.

Tasks to complete

1. Go and explore the media library. Practice uploading a photo, video, or sound file, and grabbing the URL.

2. Try using the search feature to find a specific piece of media in your library.

Pages v posts

When you want to add written content to your site, you have two options. You can either create a **Page** or a **Post**. In terms of adding/editing, these two are very similar, but they are actually quite different in terms of function.

This may sound confusing to people who are new to WordPress (or maybe even new to website building). After all, isn't a post on your site a page? Doesn't a page on your site contain a post?

For some reason, WordPress creators decided to name these two types of content "posts" and "pages" and it does cause confusion. However, you do need to understand the basic differences between them when it comes to building your site. The information I'll give you later will make it easy for you to decide which to use, so don't start panicking.

Since WordPress was originally designed as a blogging platform (i.e. to help build websites that were constantly updated with posts about whatever was going on in that blogger's life), posts were designed for these regular updates.

WordPress **posts** are *date-dependent and chronological,* and this separates them from **pages** which are date-independent and not really related to any other piece of content on the site.

Posts were originally designed to be ordered by date. A post you created yesterday should logically appear lower down the page than a post you make today. Newer posts are inserted at the top of the page, and older posts are pushed off the bottom. If you think back to the WordPress reading settings, we saw that the default homepage of a WordPress site shows posts in this manner.

A typical blog will be structured this way. Let's look at an example.

Suppose you were keeping a blog about your weight loss program. On day one you weighed in at 210lb, so you write about that and what you have done for the day to help with your diet. Each day you write a new entry as a kind of personal journey on your weight loss progress.

When someone comes to your site, they see the daily posts in chronological order. This means visitors to your 'blog' can follow your story logically and see how your diet is working out for you.

This type of chronology is not possible with pages (well it is, but it takes a lot of effort plus plugins to achieve, so why bother?). Pages do not have any defined order, though they can have a hierarchy of parent and child pages.

OK, so the date-dependency is one important difference between WordPress posts and pages. What else?

Well, posts can be categorized, pages cannot (at least not without plugins).

Suppose you were creating a site about exercise equipment. You might have a series of reviews on different treadmills, another set of reviews on exercise bikes, and so on.

Using posts allows us to categorize our content into relevant groups. If I had 10 reviews of various weight loss programs, I could create a category on my site called weight loss programs and add all 10 reviews to this category by writing them as posts.

Putting related content into the same category makes sense from a human visitor point of view, but also from the point of view of a search engine. If someone were on your site reading a review of the Hollywood Diet, it would be easy to use features of WordPress posts to highlight other reviews in the same category. This can be done with posts, but it is a much more manual process if you tried doing the same thing with pages.

Posts can also be tagged with related words and phrases.

Tags are an additional way to group and categorize your content. We'll discuss tags later, but for now, just realize that they can be used to further categorize your content to help your visitors and the search engines make sense of your project.

It is possible to create tags for pages as well, but once again, only with plugins. As a rule, we try not to use plugins unless they are essential, as they can slow down the loading time of a website, and possibly add security vulnerabilities if they are not well maintained by their creators.

Another great feature of posts is that they can have **Excerpts**. These are short descriptions of the article that can be used by themes and plugins to create a Meta description tag or a description of the article in a list of related articles. For example, below is a related posts section (created using the YARPP plugin that we'll install later), on my ezSEONews website. It shows excerpts being used for the post descriptions:

Related Posts:

1. EzSEO Newsletter #353 – Optimizing for Google's RankBrain
   How to optimize your content for Google's RankBrain and other tidbits of information....

2. SEO Tip #1–Don't write content about a keyword phrase
   SEO Tip #1 of 10....

3. SEO Tip #2–Don't publish "fluffy" content
   In this short video, I'll show you a major mistake that many marketers make – they publish content that is padded, even to the extent...

If a post does not have an excerpt (e.g. if you forgot to write one), the first X words of

121

the article itself are used for the description. Bear in mind that the first sentence or two of the article does not always make the best description for the article, so I recommend you add excerpts to all posts on your site.

Another important feature of posts is that they appear in your site's RSS feed. Remember, we talked about how important RSS feeds are, earlier in the book. Since RSS feeds are there to highlight the most recent posts, any important new content on the site should be a post, so that it appears in your feeds.

When to use posts and when to use pages

OK, this is the million-dollar question that I get asked a lot!

Not all webmasters agree on this, but I am going to give you a simple rule that will tell you when to use a post and when to use a page. I have built sites using this rule for many years, for myself, and my clients. This rule offers great SEO benefits as well as organizing content in a logical manner to help both visitors and search engines.

Before I tell you the rule, let me first distinguish between two types of content that you may have on your site.

The first type of content is your "call to action" stuff. It's the content you want your visitors to see. The content you want ranking high in Google. We will call this type of content, **Niche Content**. This will include articles, reviews, videos, infographics, etc. that **you create for your site and your targeted audience.**

The second type of content is the stuff that you need to have on the site, but from a financial point of view, you don't really care whether visitors find it. This type of content does not fit into logical groups like we saw with posts. Typical examples would be a Privacy page and Terms of Service. I'd also add the "contact" and "about us" pages to this grouping. I call this type of content my "legal pages".

Do you understand the difference?

Here is the basic rule.

Use Posts for "Niche Content", and Pages for "Legal Pages".

It's a simple enough rule, and it will make perfect sense when we start adding pages and posts to the website. Before we can do that though, we need to look at post categories and tags.

Tasks to complete

1. Go over this section until the differences between pages and posts are clear in your mind.

2. Can you make a list of any legal pages you may require on your site?

Categories & tags

Before we can start adding posts to our site, we need to think about the way the site will be structured and how the posts will be organized within the site.

We have already touched on categories and tags earlier in the book and have set up the SEO settings for these taxonomies. Let's have a closer look at categories and tags so that you can fully understand them and add a few to your site.

Both categories and tags are ways to categorize your posts.

All posts MUST be assigned to a category, but tags are optional. Categories are, therefore, more important than tags.

Think of categories as the main way to organize your posts. Think of tags as an additional organizational tool, that can be called upon if needed.

Let's look at an example.

Let's consider a website about vacuum cleaners. What would your main categories?

If you had a bunch of vacuum cleaner reviews, how would you want them organized?

Possibly more importantly, how would your website visitors expect them to be organized?

Here are some ideas for categories:

Dyson

Handheld

Dyson Ball

Eureka

Bagless

Cordless

Hoover

Upright

Canister

Miele

HEPA filter

All of these could be categories, but then you might get to the situation where one post might fit into several categories. While WordPress encourages this, I recommend you put each post into ONE category only (for SEO purposes). Forcing yourself to think of one category per post can actually help you find the best categories for your site.

Of those ideas listed above, which ones would make the most sense if a vacuum could only be in one category?

How about "bagless"?

Nope. A vacuum could be bagless, upright and a Dyson.

The obvious categories from that list would be the ones were a vacuum could only fit into one - the brand names. My categories would therefore be:

Dyson

Eureka

Hoover

Miele

A Dyson DC25 vacuum cleaner review could only go into one category – the Dyson category.

So, what about the other terms:

Handheld

Dyson Ball

Bagless

Cordless

Upright

Canister

HEPA filter

A vacuum could be cordless, bagless, and contain a HEPA filter! That's a clear indication that these features are not suited as categories, however, they are perfect as tags!

For example, my review of the Dyson DC25 vacuum would be in the category Dyson but could be tagged with ball, HEPA, bagless & upright.

The beauty of using tags is that for every tag you use, WordPress will create a page just for that tag. The tag page will list ALL posts that have been assigned that tag. In the example above, WordPress would create FOUR tag pages. One for "ball", one for "HEPA", one for "Bagless" and one for "Upright".

The "HEPA" tag page will list all vacuums on the site that have been tagged with HEPA – it helps visitors find more HEPA vacuums if that is what they are interested in.

The "Bagless" tag page would list all vacuums on the site that were bagless (and therefore tagged with that term). A visitor to my site looking for a bagless vacuum could use the tag page to quickly see all available bagless vacuums that had been reviewed to date.

Tags help the search engines too. They provide additional information about an article, helping search engines understand what the content is about.

There is no doubt that tags are powerful. However, with that power comes some responsibility. If you abuse tags, your site will become spammy.

I have seen sites where posts have been tagged with 10, 20, 50, and even several hundred tags. Don't believe me? See this screenshot showing the tags for a post on one website I came across:

You don't need to be able to read the words in that screenshot to get the point. I've had to reduce the size of the screenshot to get all the tags into view. There are over 160 tags for that single post. I happen to know that Google penalized that site.

Every tag in that list will have its own tag page.

The biggest problem for that site is that many of the tags used on that post are not used on any other posts. That means there are 100+ tag pages with just a single post listed as using that tag.

To think about this in another way, if a post lists 160 tags, and this is the only post on the website, then the site will contain over 160 pages. It'll contain one post, 160 tag pages which are all nearly identical (as they all just list the same post), and a few other pages that WordPress creates for us, which will actually be almost identical to the 160 tag pages.

The way the webmaster used tags in this example is clearly spam, and search engines hate spam. Please, use tags responsibly!

Let's look at one more example.

Think of a recipe website about puddings, desserts, cakes and so on.

You might have main categories like:

Ice cream

Cakes

Muffins

Mousse

Cookies

These are the obvious categories since a dessert will only be able to fit into one of the categories. To further classify the recipes on the site, we'd use tags which would add a little more detail about each post.

What type of tags would you use?

Stuck for ideas?

Tags usually choose themselves as you add more content to a website. For example, you might find that a lot of recipes use chocolate, or walnuts, or vanilla, or frosting (you get the idea). These would make perfect tags because a visitor with a hankering for chocolate could visit the chocolate tag page and see a list of all ice cream, cakes, muffins, mousse and cookies that include chocolate.

Do you see how the tags help with additional layers of categorization? The tag pages become useful pages for visitors.

This is the mindset you are looking to develop as you utilize tags for your own website.

A few guidelines for using tags

1. Keep a list of tags you use on your site and make sure you spell them correctly when you reuse them. Remember, if you misspell a tag, another tag page will be created for the misspelled version.

2. Don't create tags that will only apply to one post. Remember, tags are there to help classify your content into groups. Most tags will be used several times on a site, and its use will increase as you add more content. I'd recommend that you only use a tag if it will be used on 3 or more posts.

3. Only pick a small number of relevant tags per post. I'd recommend somewhere

126

between 3 – 6 tags per post, but if some need more, then that's fine. If some need less that's OK too. This is just a general rule of thumb.

4. NEVER use a tag that is also a category.

Setting up categories & tags in your dashboard

Categories and tags are properties of posts, so you'll find the menus to work with them under the **Posts** menu in the sidebar.

Categories and tags can either be set up before you start writing content, or added as you are composing it. The most common method is to set up the main categories before you begin, but add tags while you are writing your post.

I recommend that you create a description for all tags and categories, and to do that, you will need to go into **Categories** editor and **Tags** editor using the Posts menu.

OK, let's go and set up a category first. Click on the **Categories** menu:

On the right, you will see a list of current categories.

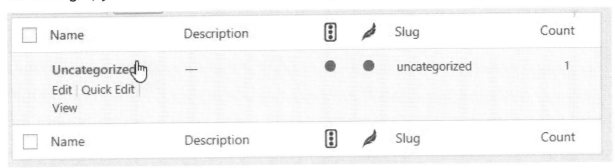

Note that two of the columns in that screenshot (readability and SEO score) were added by the Yoast SEO plugin. If you do not see those columns, you probably disabled them earlier.

There is only one category – Uncategorized. WordPress set this up for you during the WordPress installation. Since it is currently set as the default category for posts, it cannot be deleted. We could create another category and then make it the default for posts. We could then delete the Uncategorized category. However, we can just change the name of the uncategorized category so it is useful for the site.

If you mouseover the category, you'll see a menu appear under the title (see the screenshot above).

Quick Edit will allow you to change the category name AND the category slug. The slug is just the text that is used in the URL to represent the category of the post. Remember we set up Permalinks earlier to look like this:

/%category%/%postname%/

The %category% variable is replaced by the category slug and the %postname% variable will be replaced by the post name.

WordPress will automatically create the slug when you save your category. To create the category slug, WordPress uses the same text as the category name (converted to lowercase), with any spaces replaced by a dash.

Therefore, a category name of **juicer reviews** would have a default slug of **juicer-reviews**, but you can specify your own slug if you prefer not to use the WordPress default.

OK, let's edit the Uncategorized category.

Click on the **Edit** link under the **Uncategorized** name.

Edit Category

Name	Uncategorized

The name is how it appears on your site.

Slug	uncategorized

The "slug" is the URL-friendly version of the name. It is usually all lowercase and contains only letters, numbers, and hyphens.

Enter a new name for your default category, and leave the **slug** box empty, like this:

Name	Wordpress tutorial

The name is how it appears on your site.

Slug	

The "slug" is the URL-friendly version of the letters, numbers, and hyphens.

Enter a description for your category.

When you are done, scroll to the bottom of the page and click the **Update** button.

Now click the **Back to Categories** link at the top of the page:

WordPress will use **WordPress-tutorials** as the slug. That will become the text that is used in the URLs of all posts in the category.

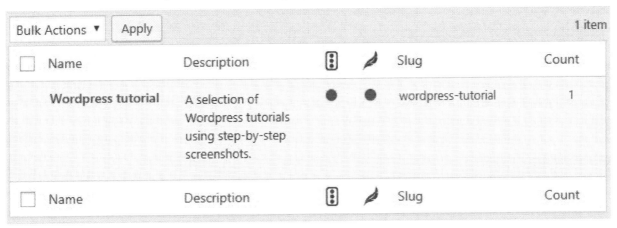

The description will be used as the Meta description of the category page.

When we were editing the category, you might have seen an option to specify a parent category. I didn't mention it at the time, as there is no "parent" for my default category, but what is a parent category?

Parent categories & hierarchy

Categories can be hierarchical. In other words, you can have categories within categories.

An example might be a website on car maintenance. I might have a category called Toyota, but then want sub-categories called Yaris, Auris, Prius, Land Cruiser, etc. etc.

Therefore, the parent category would be Toyota. When I create the Yaris, Auris, Prius, Land Cruiser categories, I'd select Toyota as the parent.

Add New Category

Name

Yaris

The name is how it appears on your site.

Slug

The "slug" is the URL-friendly version of the name. It is usually all lowercase and contains only letters, numbers, and hyphens.

Parent

Toyota ▼

Categories, unlike tags, can have a hierarchy. You might have a Jazz category, and under that have children categories for Bebop and Big Band. Totally optional.

In the list of categories, you can spot parent/child relationships because parent category is listed first, with the child categories indented below:

	Name	Description	Slug	C
☐	**Toyota**		toyota	
☐	— Land Cruiser		land-cruiser	
☐	— Prius		prius	
☐	— Auris		auris	
☐	— Yaris		yaris	

Parent/Child categories are very useful for tidying up the navigation menus on your site.

Imagine if you had 10 different cars from each of 5 manufacturers. That would be 50 categories for your site. That is a lot of categories to display in a menu!

By using parent-child categories, you can just have the 5 main manufacturers in your menu, with the model of the cars only visible when selecting its parent.

Adding a new category

Adding a new category is easy.

Click the **Categories** menu from inside the **Posts** menu.

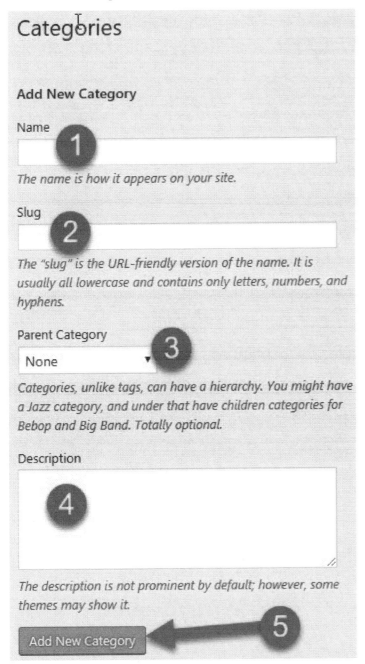

Fill in the name, slug (if you want to), and a description. Then select a parent if applicable. Click the **Add New Category** button and your new category is ready for use.

OK, let's look at the Yoast SEO settings for categories.

Click on **Categories** in the **Posts** menu.

Move your mouseover a category and click the **edit** link.

Scroll to the bottom of the screen, and you'll see the Yoast SEO settings.

These settings are added by the Yoast SEO plugin that we set up earlier.

This is what you'll see:

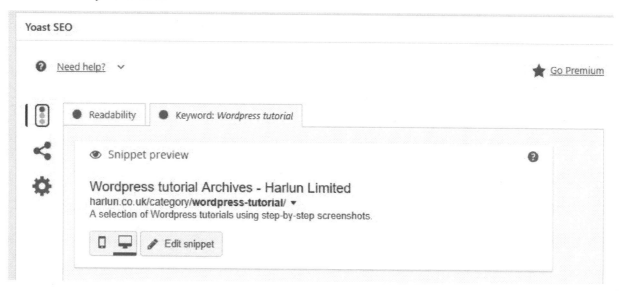

There may be tabs across the top labeled **Readability** and **Keyword,** as shown in the screenshot. You may also see a **Focus keyword** section. I switched these off earlier in the book, but if you are seeing them, let me remind you how to switch them off, as you don't need this extra clutter.

Click on **Dashboard** inside the **SEO** sidebar menu and select the **Features** tab.

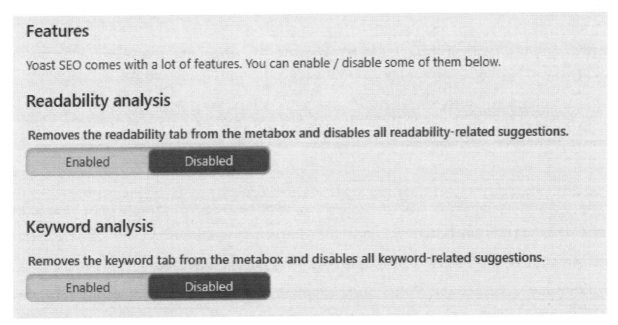

Features

Yoast SEO comes with a lot of features. You can enable / disable some of them below.

Readability analysis

Removes the readability tab from the metabox and disables all readability-related suggestions.

| Enabled | Disabled |

Keyword analysis

Removes the keyword tab from the metabox and disables all keyword-related suggestions.

| Enabled | Disabled |

Disable **Readability analysis** and **Keyword analysis** and **Save changes.** If you decide you want to explore these features later, you know where to turn them back on.

OK, go back to **Categories** inside the **Posts** menu.

You will notice that the readability and keyword columns are no longer there in the table of categories.

Click **Edit** under one of your categories and scroll back down to the Yoast SEO settings.

You now have fewer options:

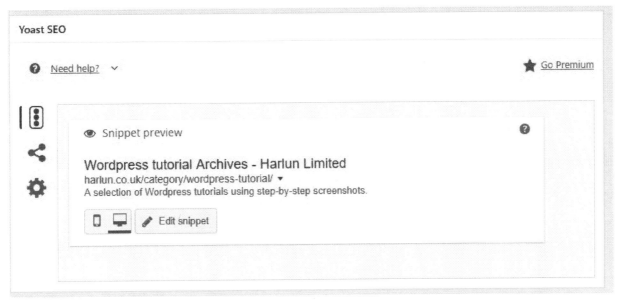

What you can see in the snippet editor is a snapshot of what your category page will look like on Google. You can see the title of the category page, URL, and description (which is one reason we added a description to the category when we created it).

On the left, you can see three buttons. The top one gives you access to this snippet editor. Click the **Edit Snippet** button to open all the editing options for the category.

You'll see you can change the SEO title and Meta Description using variables we looked at when setting up the Yoast SEO plugin. You are not restricted to using variables - you can type whatever you want in there. You can also edit the slug if you decide you want to.

The second button on the left is the **Share** screen, offering some settings for Facebook and Twitter. If you want to control what is written on Facebook and Twitter if someone shares the category page, then you can do so here.

The third button on the left gives you access to some useful settings.

At the top, you can see the **Meta Robots Index** drop-down box. This allows you to tell the search engines either to index the category page, or not. The default will be taken from the global settings we set up earlier. You should leave this default setting.

You have the option to exclude the category page from the sitemap. Again, we can leave this as the default **Auto Detect**.

Ignore the **Canonical URL** option -we'll let WordPress take care of that for us.

If you made any changes, be sure to click the **Update** button to save them.

Adding Tags

Adding Tags is very similar to adding categories except tags cannot have a parent-child relationship with each other.

For every tag you enter, add a description to explain what that tag is being used for. That description will then be used for the Meta description of the tag page; this is how we set it up within the SEO plugin, remember?

Like the categories, the **Add Tag** screen has just a few options - Title, Slug, and Description. You only need to fill in the Title and Description because WordPress will handle the slug for us. However, if you go in and edit an existing tag, you will see extra Yoast SEO settings for the tag. These are identical settings to the Category edit screen but do go in and have a look.

While I expect you will add tags directly on the **Add Post** screen as you write your content, I do highly recommend you come back to this section every time you use a new tag, just to fill in a description for those tags you create. When you make a new tag on the **Add Post** screen, you don't have the option of adding the description there and then, but it is important to add one nonetheless.

Tasks to complete

1. Set up a few categories for your site.
2. Think about possible tags and keep a list on a notepad.
3. Make sure to add descriptions to every tag and category that you add.

Writing posts

Whether you are writing posts or pages, the main content editor is the same.

To create a new post on your site, click **Add New** in the **Posts** menu.

The **Add New Post** (and **Add New Page**) screen has a lot of information on it. Let's look at the What You See Is What You Get (WYSIWYG) Editor first.

WordPress WYSIWYG editor

The toolbar of the editor (the place where you add your content), looks like this:

If you only see one line of buttons on your toolbar, click the **Toggle Toolbar** button on the right. That will expand the toolbar.

You'll see on the top right there are two tabs - **Visual & Text**.

The Visual tab is where you can write your content using WYSIWYG features. On this tab, you'll see text and media formatted as it will appear on the website once published. This is the tab you will want to use for most of the work you do when adding new, or editing existing content, on your site.

The other tab - Text - shows the raw code that is responsible for the layout and content of the page. Unless you specifically need to insert some code or script into your content, stick with the Visual tab.

The two rows of buttons allow you to format your content visually. If you have used any type of Word Processor before, then this should be intuitive.

I won't go through the functions of all these buttons. If you need help understanding what a button does, move your mouseover it to get a popup help tooltip.

Adding content to your site is as easy as typing it into the large box under the toolbar. Just use it like you would any word processor.

Write your content. Select some text and click a formatting button to apply the format. Make it bold, or change its color, make it a header, or any of the other features offered in the toolbar.

To create a headline, enter the headline and press the return button on your keyboard to make sure it is on its own line. Now click somewhere in the headline and select the headline from the drop-down box in the toolbar.

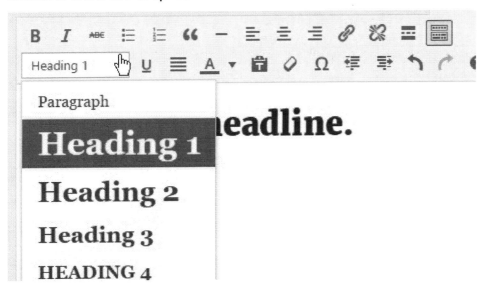

NOTE: WordPress themes typically show the title of your post as an H1 header at the top of the page. This is the biggest header available and is equivalent to the **Heading1** in the drop-down selector. You should not use more than one H1 header on a web page, so avoid using the **Heading 1** as you write your content. Use **Heading 2** for main sections within your article, and **Heading 3** for sub-headers inside **Heading 2** sections.

OK, it's now time to go ahead and write the post, for your website.

As you write your article, you may want to insert an image or some other form of media. We looked at the Media library earlier in the book, but let's go through the process of adding an image to an article.

Adding images

The process is straightforward.

Position your cursor in the article where you want to add the image. Don't worry too much about getting it in the right place because you can always re-position it later if you need to.

Click the **Add Media** button located above the WYSIWYG editor, to the left, and you'll see the popup screen that we've seen previously:

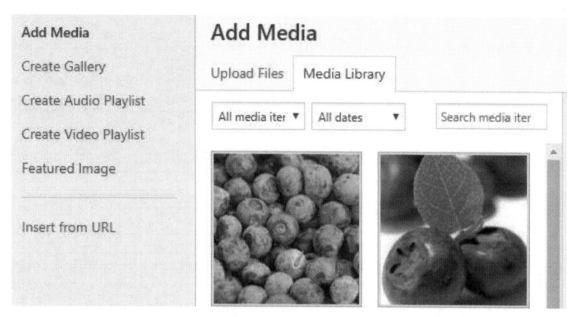

From this screen, you can select an image from the media library, or click the **Upload Files** tab to upload a new image to the media library.

Let's add an image from our Media Library.

Click the **Media Library** tab if it is not already selected and click on the image you want to use in the post.

A check mark appears in the top right corner of the image, and the "attachment" details are displayed on the right side. These image details can be edited if you want to.

At the bottom of the right sidebar is an **Insert into post** button. Before you click that, we should consider a few of the sidebar options.

One important option is the **Alt Text**. This text is read to the visually impaired visitors on your site and helps them understand what images are being shown. Therefore, add a short descriptive ALT text. For my example, **blueberries** is sufficient.

At the bottom of the right-hand column are some **Attachment Display Settings**. Currently, my image is set to "none" for alignment.

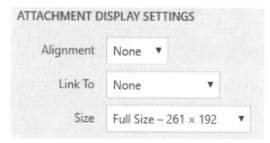

I want to align the image to the left so can select that from the drop-down box. When an image is aligned left (or right) in WordPress, the post text wraps around it. If you select **None** or **Center** for alignment, the text won't wrap.

The next option you have is to link your image to something. The default setting is **None**, meaning we insert an image that is not clickable by the visitor because it is not linked to anything. This is the setting I use on 99% of all images I embed in posts.

You can link an image to a **Media File, Attachment page** or **Custom URL.**

The one that I think you will find the most useful is the **Custom** URL. This allows you to navigate to a URL when a user clicks an image. For example, if your image is a "Buy Now" button, you'd want the image linked to the purchase page.

The last of the display settings is **Size.** You'll be able to choose from **Full size** and **thumbnail.** The dimensions are included with each file size, so choose the one that is closest to the size you want the image to appear on your page.

I want my image to be full sized (as I had resized the image to the correct size before I uploaded it to the media library), so I'd select **Full Size.**

Once you have made your selection, click the **Insert into post** button at the bottom.

Here is that image inserted into my post at the position of my cursor:

condimentum gravida. Nunc finibus risus et bibendum cursus. Ut ut libero vitae odio hendrerit varius sed eu tortor.

Fusce malesuada aliquam dolor, eu sagittis elit cursus nec. Etiam nec dictum ante. Vivamus tempor finibus ipsum, ac elementum diam facilisis nec. Nulla laoreet ex a ullamcorper eleifend. Sed fermentum velit dui, eget semper nulla fermentum vel. Nunc id sagittis mauris, non

If you have the position wrong, you can simply click the image to select it, and drag the image to a different location.

If you find that the image isn't inserted as you intended (e.g. you forgot to align it), click on the image. A toolbar appears above the image and a bounding box around it:

The bounding box includes a small square in each corner. You can use this to resize the image. Drag one of the corners to make the image bigger or smaller.

The first 4 buttons in the toolbar allow you to re-align the image.

The last button in the toolbar will delete the image.

The toolbar edit button looks like a pencil. You can use this to open the **Image Details** screen to make a number of changes:

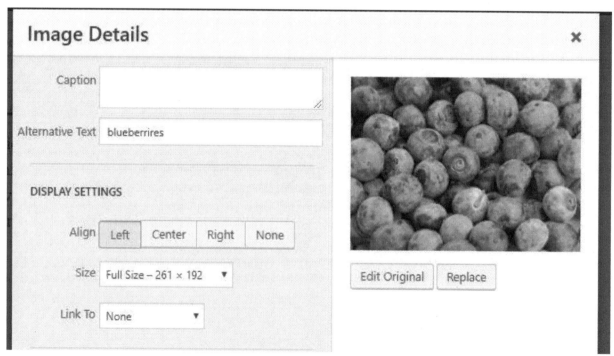

You'll also see a link to **Advanced Options** at the bottom. Click that to expand the advanced options:

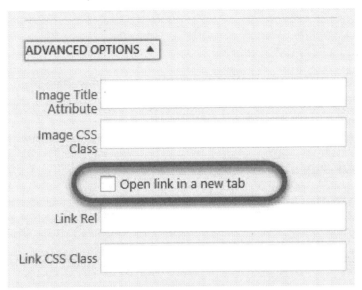

The advanced option that is most useful to us is the **Open link in a new tab** option. When someone clicks the image, whatever it is linked to opens in a new browser tab.

Once you have made your edits on this screen, click the **Update** button and the changes will be updated in your post.

You can insert videos from your Media library in the same way.

OK, finish your first post.

Something to try: We added an image that was already in the Media Library. Go ahead and add an image from your hard disk. After clicking the Add Media button, you'll need to go to the Upload tab to proceed. Try it and see if you can successfully add an image this way.

Once you've done that, try adding an image to a post by dragging and dropping the image from your computer directly into the WYSIWYG editor window.

It's all very intuitive.

There are a few things we need to do before we publish a post, so let's go through the complete sequence from start, to publish:

   1. Add a post title.
   2. Write & format your post using the visual text editor (WYSIWYG).
   3. Select a post format if available. You can ignore this option for most posts you add.
   4. Select a category.
   5. Add some tags if you want to. Tags can always be added later, so don't feel under any pressure to add them now. Of course, you can also decide you don't want

to use tags on your site. That is fine too.

  6. Add an excerpt.
  7. Select a date/time if you want to schedule the post for the future.
  8. Publish/Schedule the post.

OK, so far we have completed down to step 2.

Post format

Not all WordPress themes use Post Formats. The Twenty Sixteen theme that we are using does and you can see them on the right of your screen:

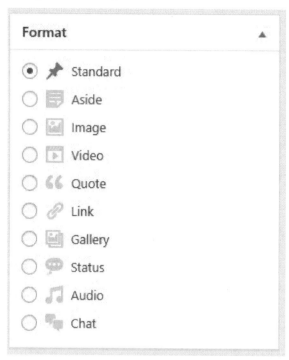

Since most, if not all your posts, should use the default (Standard), we won't go into details in this book about other formats. Most people just won't use them and not all themes support them.

If you are interested in post formats, experiment with them. Select one and update your post. Then view your post to see how it looks. You can also read more about Post Formats on the WordPress websites:

http://codex.WordPress.org/Post_Formats

Post Category

The next step in our publishing sequence is to choose a category. Choose just one category for each post.

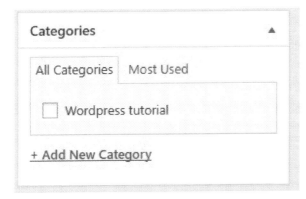

If you forget to check a category box, WordPress will automatically use your default category.

You can add a new category "on the fly" from within the **Add post** screen, but if you do, remember to go in and write a description for the new category so it can be used as the meta description of that category page (remember the Yoast SEO plugin we set up earlier is expecting a description of categories and tags).

Post Tags

If you want to use tags for the post, you can type them directly into the tags box, even if they don't already exist. When you are finished typing the tags, click the **Add** button to the right of the tags box.

As you add and use more tags, you can click on the link **Choose from the most used tags** and a box will appear with some of the tags you've used before. You can just click the tags that apply and they'll be added to the tag list of your post.

If you add new tags when entering a post, remember to go into the Tags settings to write a short description for each one. Yes, it takes time. However, this will be used as the Meta description of the tag page.

Post Excerpt

You should add a post excerpt to all posts. If you don't see an excerpt entry box on your screen, check the **Screen Options** to make sure **Excerpt** is checked.

Once checked, the **Excerpt** box magically appears on your edit post screen.

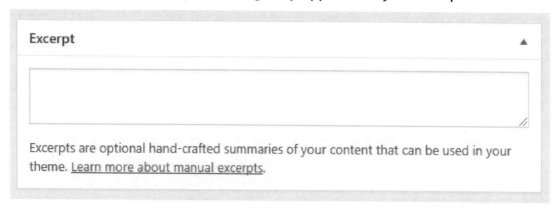

The excerpt should be a short description of the post you are writing. Its purpose is to encourage visitors to click through and read the article (e.g. From the search engine). This excerpt will be used as the Meta description tag of the post, as well as the description of the post in the "related posts" section, which is displayed at the end of each article you publish (see the YARPP plugin later).

Enter a three to five sentence excerpt that encourages the click.

Publishing the Post

The next step in the process is deciding when you want the post to go live on your site. Let's look at the **Publish** section of the screen.

The first option you have is to save the post as a draft.

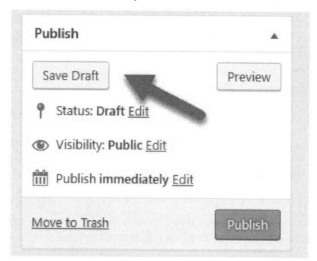

Once saved as a draft, you can go back at any time to make changes or publish the article. Draft posts are not shown on your site. To be visible on your website, you need to publish the post.

If you want it up there immediately, then click the Publish button. If like me, you are writing several posts in a batch, it is a good idea to spread the posting of the content out a little bit. Luckily, WordPress allows us to schedule the posts into the future.

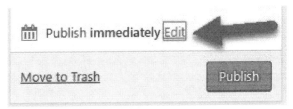

The default is to publish **immediately**. However, there is an **Edit** link you can click to open a scheduling calendar:

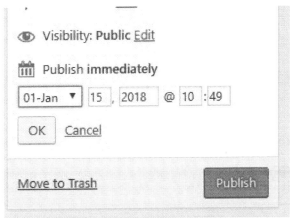

Enter the date and time you want to publish the post and then click the OK button.

The publish button now changes to **Schedule**.

Click the **Schedule** button to schedule the post.

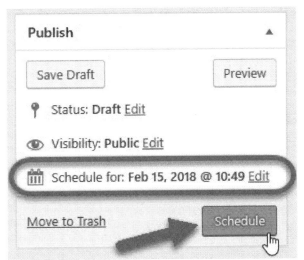

That's it. You've just published or scheduled your first WordPress post.

Yoast SEO Settings for the Post

Before we move on, there is one last thing to cover here. It's the way that the Yoast SEO plugin is integrated into the **Add New Post** (and **Add New Page**), screen. We did look briefly at this when setting up the plugin.

If you scroll down a little, you should come across the **Yoast SEO** section.

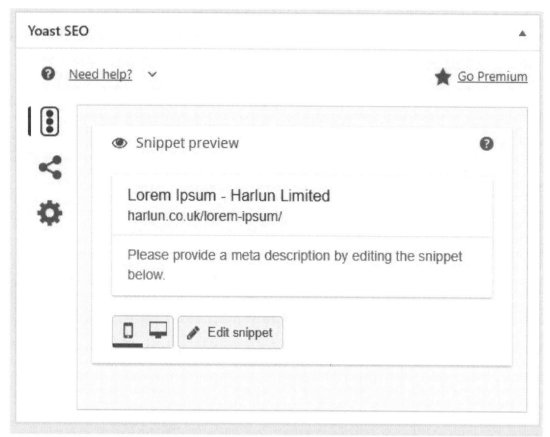

NOTE: If you don't see this section, make sure it is checked in the screen options (top right).

This Yoast SEO box looks very similar to the ones we saw for category and tag pages. The big difference is in the **Advanced** settings screen, which you access by clicking the third button down on the left (the "cog").

These settings give us fine control over how the search engines will deal with this post. We can use these settings to override the global settings for the site. This is powerful. With this fine level of control, we can treat every post and page on our site differently if we want to.

The top setting is **Meta Robot Index**. By default, all posts will be indexed. If we don't want a post indexed and visible in the search engines, we can select **noindex** from the drop-down box. However, this would be most unusual for posts.

The next setting is the **Meta Robots Follow** option. This defines whether we want search engines to follow the links in the post. The default is yes, but we can set them to nofollow. I don't recommend changing this unless you know what you are doing.

The **Meta Robots Advanced** allows us to set a few other Meta tags on our pages. Click on the edit box where it currently says **Site-wide default: None** and a drop-down box appears with options you can set:

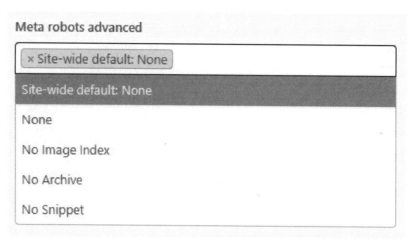

No Image Index is useful if you don't want the search engines to index the images on your page. Indexed images can be easily found within the image search on Google, and pirated.

No Archive tag tells Google not to store a cached copy of your page

No Snippet tells Google not to show a description under your Google listing (nor will it show a cached link in the search results).

The only options you may want to add occasionally is the **No Archive** option, but only in very special circumstances. There are times when we don't want Google to keep an archive (cached version), of a page. By setting the post as **No Archive** we are preventing the search engines from keeping a backup of the page.

Why might you want to do this?

Well, maybe you have a limited offer on your site and you don't want people seeing it after the offer has finished. If the page was archived, it is technically possible for someone to go in and see the last cached page at Google, which will still show your previous offer.

Editing posts

At some point after writing a post, you may want to go in and edit or update it. This is an easy process. Just click on **All Posts** in the **Posts** menu. It will open a screen with a list of posts on your site.

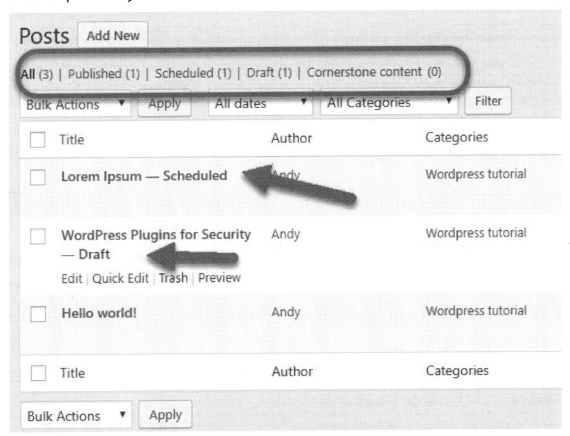

In the screenshot, you can see that I have three posts on the site. The top one is scheduled, the second one is a draft, and the third one is published.

You can view just the published, just the scheduled, or just the draft posts, by clicking on the item in the menu at the top.

What if you had a lot of posts and needed to find one?

There are two ways of doing this. One is from within your Dashboard using the available search and filtering tools. The other method is one I'll show you later and involves visiting your site while you are logged into the Dashboard.

For now, let's look at how we can find posts from within the Dashboard:

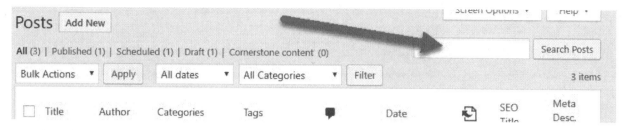

Firstly, if you know what month you wrote the post, you could show all posts from that month by selecting the month from the **All Dates** drop-down box. You can also search for a post by showing just those posts within a certain category. Select the desired category from the **All Category** drop-down box.

Perhaps the easiest way of all is to use the **Search Posts** feature. Type in a keyword phrase you know is in the title and then click the **Search Posts** button.

Once the list of matching posts is displayed, mouseover the one you want to edit and click edit from the popup menu. An even easier way is to just click the title of the post. This takes you back to the same editor screen you used when first creating the post. Make your changes in there and just click the **Update** button to save your modifications.

NOTE: Whenever you make changes to a post, WordPress keeps a record (archive), of those changes. At the bottom of your Add/Edit post screen is a section called **Revisions**.

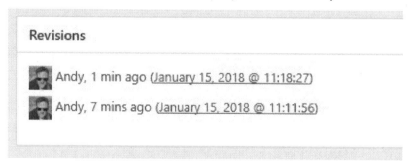

If you don't see it, make sure it is checked in the screen options from the top. You also won't see this section if you haven't made changes to the post.

The revisions list shows all the changes that have been made to a post, including the time stamp and the user that made the edits.

You can view any previous version of the post by clicking the date link. You won't lose the current version; it just opens a viewing screen so you can see what that previous version looked like. If I click on the last revision at the top of the list (i.e. the one before the currently saved version), I see this:

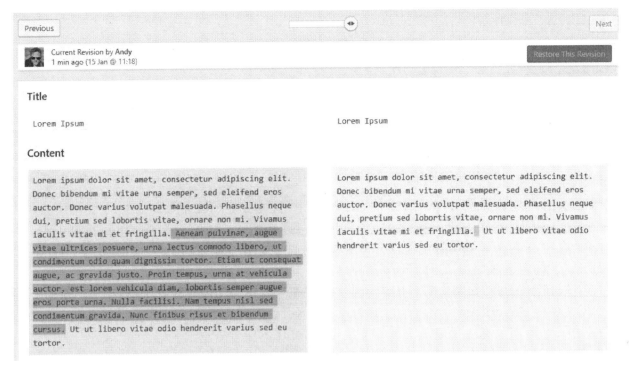

There is a link in the top left of the screen to take you back to the post editor. Click this link if you want to cancel and return to the editor.

Below this, you can see two different versions of the post. There is one on the left and one on the right. These are in chronological order, with the oldest on the left, newest on the right. The previous revision is therefore on the left, the current saved post on the right.

The differences between the two versions will be highlighted in yellow on the right (and red on the left).

At the top of the screen, you will also see a slider.

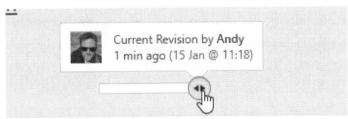

Move the slider left or right to scroll through the revisions.

Why use revisions?

Suppose you are working on a post and delete a paragraph or change an image. Later, you ask yourself "why did I delete that?". With revisions, you can revert to previous versions of your post with a few mouse clicks.

Restoring a revision

If you find a revision you want to restore, it's as simple as clicking the **Restore This Revision** button.

This will copy the post into the editor as it was when the revision was saved, but also create a new revision of the post you are over-writing (that means you won't lose anything). When the revision is restored, you are back on the **Post Edit** screen, but nothing is saved until you click the **Update** button.

Tasks to complete

1. Enter a post. It doesn't have to be a real post and you can always delete it afterward. I just want you to feel comfortable using the WYSIWYG editor. Add text and an image, and then play around with the image alignment and settings.

2. Publish your post and go to your site to see how it looks in your web browser.

3. Go back and edit the post and resave (to create a revision). Repeat this a few times making changes to the post each time you do.

4. Now scroll to the bottom of the page and look at the revisions section. Check out the differences between two revisions of your post. Use the slider to scroll through the revisions. Try reinstating an earlier version and then change it back again.

Making it easy for visitors to socially share your content

Having great content on your site is one thing but getting people to see it is something else.

One of the ways people find a website is through the search engines. If we rank well enough for a particular search term, the web searcher may land on our page.

Another way people can find our content is via social media channels. Places like Facebook, Google Plus, and Twitter are good examples. To make this more likely, we need to install a social sharing plugin on the site. A social sharing plugin will add buttons to the website that allow people to share the content they are reading with their followers. Social sharing buttons make sharing easy, and therefore more likely.

There are several good social sharing plugins and I do recommend you look around to find one that matches the design of your website. However, to get you started, let's install my current favorite.

Go to **Add New** in the **Plugins** menu. Search for **Social Pug** and look for this one:

Install and activate the plugin.

You'll then find the settings for the plugin inside the **Social Pug** menu in the sidebar.

Click that menu to be taken to the settings screen.

This plugin offers you two design options.

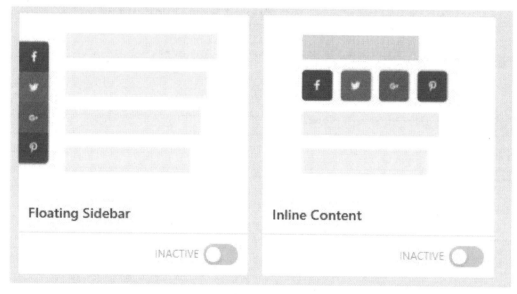

Floating Sidebar

Inline Content

The floating sidebar will create a panel on your web page, which "floats" down the side of your content and is always visible. The inline content option will insert the buttons before and/or after the article on your web page.

Currently, both are inactive. To activate one or both, click the slider button for that option and then click on the "cog" button that appears:

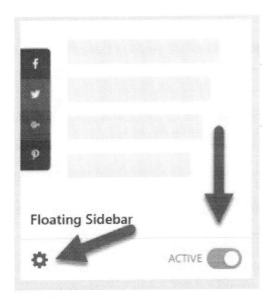

Floating Sidebar

The first thing you'll need to do is select which social sharing networks you want to offer your visitors. On the settings screen, click the **Select Networks** button, and place a checkmark next to the networks you want:

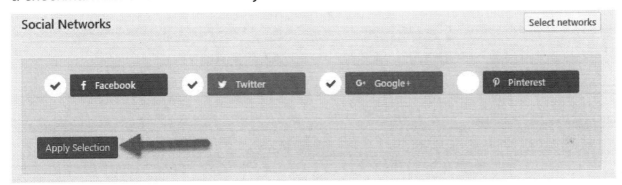

Click the **Apply Selection** button.

The networks will now appear on the settings screen, and you can re-order these by dragging them up or down using the "handle" on the left. You can also delete a network by clicking the "X" on the right.

Below you'll see some display settings. I'll leave you to explore these options. When you are ready, make sure that **Post** is checked under the **Post type display settings**, and Page is unchecked. Click **Save Changes**.

If you visit your site, you should now see the social sharing buttons. If you chose floating sidebar, it looks like this:

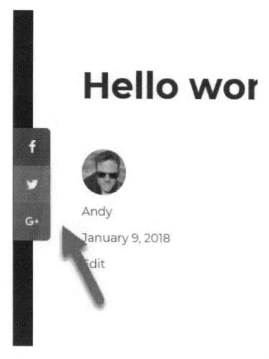

Hello wor

Andy

January 9, 2018

Edit

If you chose the inline content, it will look like this:

Hello world!

Andy

January 9, 2018

Edit

Sharing is caring!

f Facebook   🐦 Twitter   G+ Google+

Welcome to WordPress. This is your first post. Edit or delete it, then start writing!

Obviously, yours won't look exactly like mine as it depends on the settings you chose.

Other social share plugins

Over the years I have tried lots of social sharing plugins. Some work great, while others only seem to work on some websites and not others. If you find the Social Pug plugin does not work properly on *your* site, just search for "social share" in the **Add Plugins** screen, and try some.

Tasks to complete

1. Install a social sharing plugin and set it up to suit your needs.

Differences with pages

As we discussed earlier, pages are different to posts. On the Add/Edit Page screen, it all looks very similar, but there are a few notable omissions – namely no categories or tags! There is also no box to add an excerpt. These are no great loss to us, as we don't use pages for important articles/content on the site.

We do, however, have a couple of options for pages that are not found in posts – Page Attributes:

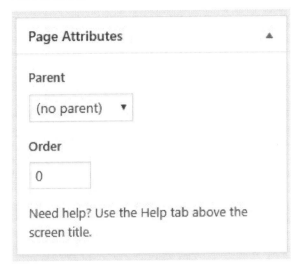

Since we are only using pages for our "legal" content (plus contact and about us), these new settings don't really apply to our site.

Since we won't be using this, I recommend you remove the page attributes box from the page edit screen.

How?

Hint: Screen Options.

Tasks to complete

1. Go and look at the page edit screen. Note the page attributes box.
2. Use the Screen Options to remove the Page Attributes box from this screen.

Internal linking of posts

One of the best ways of keeping visitors on your site is to interlink your web pages. There are a few ways of doing this.

The basic way to add a link in your content is to highlight the word or phrase that you want to use as the link's text, and then click on the link button in the toolbar:

psum dolor sit amet, consectetur adipiscing elit. Donec bibendum
: urna semper, sed eleifend eros au   r. Donec varius volutpat
ada. Phasellus neque dui,   um sed lobortis vitae, ornare non mi.
s iaculis vitae mi   ngilla. Ut ut libero vitae odio hendrerit varius
ortor.

A popup box will appear next to the highlighted word or phrase:

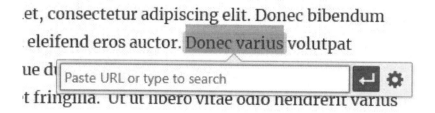

If you want to link to a webpage on a different website, paste the URL into the box.

If you want to link to a post/page on your website, type in part of the title of the webpage and WordPress will find it for you:

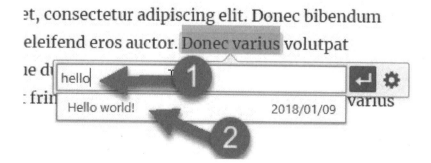

Click the post/page in the list that you want to link to. This sets the URL in the URL box. To accept the link, you can click the "Apply" button. However, before you do, you might want to change the settings of the link. To do this, click the settings button (the cog). This gives you the option to update your link details:

Insert/edit link ✕

Enter the destination URL

URL | http://harlun.co.uk/wordpress-tutorial/hello-world/

Link Text | Donec varius

☐ Open link in a new tab

Or link to existing content

Search |

No search term specified. Showing recent items.

Contact	PAGE
Sample Page	PAGE
Hello world!	2018/01/09

A useful option here is to check **Open link in a new tab**. This is something I recommend you do if linking to another website. That way, your visitor will remain on your site, and the link target will open in a new browser window for them.

When you are happy, click the **Update** button and the link will appear in the text:

t amet, consectetur adipiscing elit. Donec bibendum
, sed eleifend eros auctor. Donec varius volutpat
neque dui, pretium sed lobortis vitae, ornare non mi.
mi et fringilla. Ut ut libero vitae odio hendrerit varius

If you want to edit a link, you can do this simply by clicking it.

consectetur adipiscing elit. Donec bibendum

eifend eros auctor. Donec varius volutpa

dui, harlun.co.uk/...dpress-tutorial/hello-world ✏ ✂

ingilla. Ut ut libero vitae odio hendrerit varius

Clicking the edit button allows you to change the link. Note that there is an "unlink" button there too, which you can use if you want to remove the link altogether.

OK, that's the 100% manual way of inter-linking your web pages.

Related Posts with YARPP

One way I recommend you inter-link your content is with a plugin called **Yet Another Related Posts** plugin. This plugin allows you to set up a "Related Articles" section at the end of your posts. This will automatically create links to related articles on your site.

Go to the **Add New** Plugin screen and search for **yarpp**.

Install and activate the plugin.

You will now find the YARPP settings in the main settings menu:

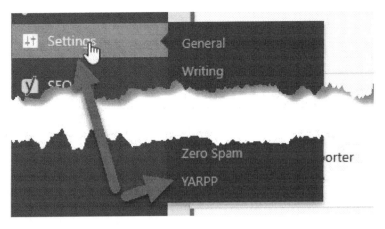

Click on **YARPP** so we can set this up.

At the top of the YARPP settings, is "The Pool". The pool is the set of posts that can be used for building a related articles section. If you decide you don't want any posts in a particular category showing up in the related articles sections on your site, you can exclude that category here by checking the box next to that category.

I am going to leave the pool defaults as they are.

If you think you won't be changing these settings, you can hide "The Pool" by unchecking the option in the **Display Settings.**

The next settings on the page are the "Relatedness" options. This defines how closely related an article needs to be, to be shown as a "related post".

I recommend you leave the relatedness options with their default values. The only change I make on smaller sites is to change the Match Threshold to a 1. On larger sites, a 2 is OK.

Next up are the **Display options for your website**.

There is plenty of scope for playing around here as well, including using your own template, but we are going to again use the default settings, with one exception. Place a checkmark next to **Show Excerpt?** This will give our related posts a description, which is taken from the excerpt we write. When you check that box, a few more options appear. Change Excerpt length to 25.

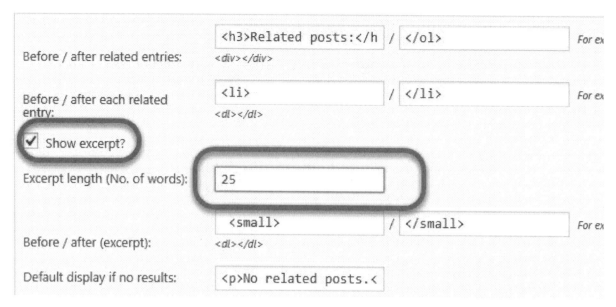

Ok, that is all we are changing. Scroll to the bottom and click **Save Changes**.

You will now have a related posts section at the end of every post on the site. You probably won't see much yet because you don't have content on the site. Here is what I see at the end of my post on this demo site:

Sharing is caring!

Welcome to WordPress. This is your first post. Edit or delete it, then start writing!

No related posts.

However, as you start adding content, the related posts section will start to populate with recommendations for your visitors.

Here is an example of a related posts section on one of my sites using this plugin.

Related Posts:

1. <u>January 2016 Google Algorithm Updates</u>
   January 2016 saw some major updates in Google, with wild swings in the rankings of many sites. What do we know about this update?...

2. <u>Google Penguin, and other Google News</u>
   Google's Penguin 4.0 is coming soon. What can you expect and how can you get ready for it?...

3. <u>Finding Hot Niches</u>
   If you have ever had problems identifying niches, or you have built a site that you thought would be profitable, and its wasn't, then Gary Harvey might have the answer with his latest offering – "Finding Hot Niches". This site is dedicated to showing you the best resources for researching...

This "related posts" section was on an article about search engine optimization on my ezSEONews.com site. Can you see the benefits? People who are reading the main SEO article are shown other articles that are related to what they've just been reading about. It gives us another chance to keep the visitor on our site.

We have looked at two ways we can inter-link our content. Firstly, we can manually create links in the content. Secondly, we can use a plugin like YARPP to show related posts to our visitors.

The last option I like to use is a plugin that I can set up to control internal linking on an automated basis, but without losing control over the linking.

I have written an article on internal site linking using this plugin. If you are interested, you should read that article here:

http://ezseonews.com/backlinks/internal-linking-seo/

Tasks to complete

1. Go and edit an existing post or create one for this exercise. Manually add a few links on this page. They can be links to pages on your site, or another website entirely.

2. Open the page in a web browser and check that the links you added work properly.

3. Install YARPP and configure it. As you add more content to your website, check out the related posts section (found at the end of every post).

The homepage of your site - blog or static?

WordPress is a tool that was originally created as a blogging platform (publishing date-related content as posts). The way in which WordPress handles these posts by default is to post them on the homepage, with the latest post at the top of that page.

In the settings, we saw that we could define how many posts to include on a page with the default set at 10. That means the last 10 posts published on the site will show up on the homepage in chronological order, with the latest post at the top and older posts below. As you post more content on the site, the older posts scroll off the bottom of the homepage and are replaced by the newer ones at the top.

If that is the type of site you want, then that's fine. You can ignore this section and leave things at their default settings.

Personally, I like to create a homepage that always displays the content I want my visitors to see on the homepage. In fact, I create a "homepage article" describing the main point of the site and helping visitors with navigation.

The good news is that creating this type of "static" homepage in WordPress is easy.

Create a WordPress "page" (not a post) and write your homepage content. Publish the page and then go to the **Reading** settings inside the **Settings** menu.

At the top of the screen, there are two radio buttons with **Your latest posts** selected as default. You need to select the **Static page** option.

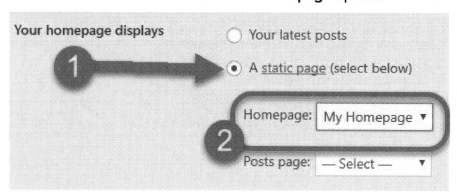

Two drop-down boxes will appear. The top one labeled **Homepage** is the one we are interested in. Click on the drop-down box and select the page you created with your homepage article. I've called mine "My Homepage" to make it clear in this example that this will be the homepage. You should give your homepage article a useful, real title because it will appear as the headline at the top of your homepage.

At the bottom of your page, click on the **Save Changes** button.

OK, you are all set. Go to your homepage and you'll see the main article being displayed. Here is mine:

Harlun Limited

Company Website

My Homepage

Homepage content here

Edit

Harlun Limited / Proudly powered by WordPress

I haven't added any content to the homepage, other than "Homepage content here", so that needs to be done. However, I think you can see how easy it is to create this type of static page for the homepage of your website.

No matter how many posts you add to your site, that homepage will not change (unless you change it).

OK, I hear your question.

"If the homepage just shows the same article, how are people going to find all my other web pages?"

Well, that's where the sidebar, widgets and custom menus come in. We'll look at those next.

Tasks to complete

1. If you want your homepage to show the same article, create a PAGE with that article. Edit the **Reading** settings to show that page on your **Homepage.**

Widgets

Widgets are basically plugins that allow you to easily add visual and interactive components to your site without needing any technical knowledge.

If you want to add a list of recent posts, you can do it easily by using a widget. Perhaps you want to add a poll to your site? Well, that can be done with widgets too.

When a designer creates a WordPress theme, their initial drawing will probably have "widgetized" blocks drawn onto it, so that they can visualize which areas will accept widgets. Maybe it will look something like this (with the shaded areas able to accept the widgets):

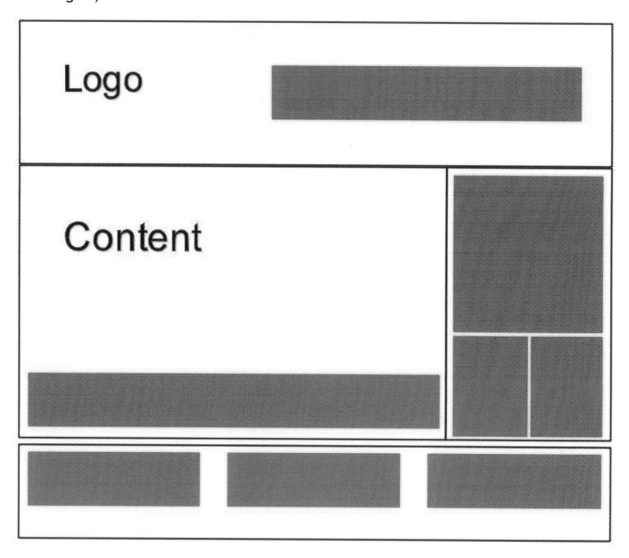

The usual areas that accept widgets are the header, sidebars, and footer. Sometimes you can also add widgets after a post content.

We'll have a look at the standard widgets that come with WordPress in a moment, but first, let's see which areas of the Twenty Sixteen theme can take widgets.

Login to your Dashboard and go to **Widgets** in the **Appearance** menu.

This will take you to an area where you can set up the widgets on your website. On the right, you'll see the collapsible rectangles we looked at earlier. These represent the areas on the site that can accept widgets. As I have mentioned before, this will be different for each theme, but for the Twenty Sixteen theme, this is what we've got to work with:

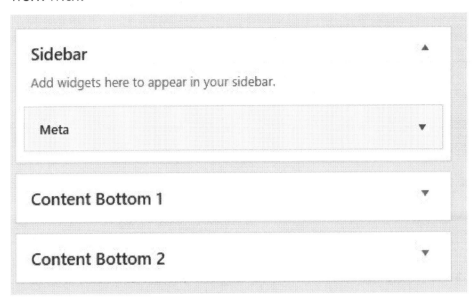

There are 3 areas of the website that can accept widgets.

Sidebar: That's the right-hand sidebar that appears on all web pages of your site.

You'll notice that there is already a widget in that area of my site. It's called **Meta**, and that adds some links to the main sidebar that you can see below:

META

- Site Admin
- Log out
- Entries RSS
- Comments RSS
- WordPress.org

If you remember, when we were clearing out the pre-installed widgets, I left that one so I could have a quick-link to log in to my website. If I wanted to remove those links from my site, I'd simply delete that widget.

The other two widgetized areas on the Twenty Sixteen theme are Content Bottom 1 and Content Bottom 2. These represent areas on the left and right, situated below the content. If you want to see these areas, add a widget to the area and load a page in your browser.

To add a widget to a widgetized area, simply drag a widget from the left and drop it in the correct area on the right. On dropping the widget, it will open out with some settings you can change. Here is the category widget:

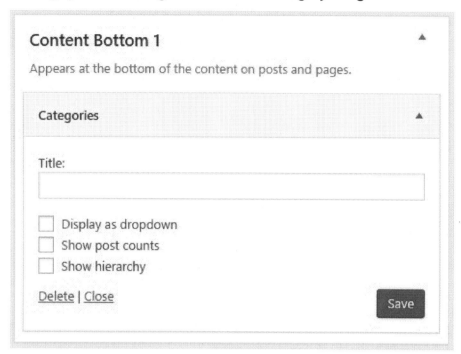

Note we can add a title. If you leave this blank, WordPress usually inserts a default title (in this case, it would be categories).

This widget also has a few settings to change the appearance of the widget. E.g. do you want categories displayed in a drop-down box? Do you want categories to show how many posts per category (this is done by showing a number in brackets)? You can also show "hierarchy" so that sub-categories are indented under their parent.

Most widgets have settings, so add a few widgets, see what they do, and see what settings they have. When playing around to see what widgets do and how they appear on your site, I recommend filling in all the settings for the widget. This will allow us to see how the WordPress template handles the formatting of the title and the text.

Here are the widgets I currently have installed in my Dashboard:

Available Widgets

To activate a widget drag it to a sidebar or click on it. To deactivate a widget and delete its settings, drag it back.

Widget	Description	Widget	Description
Archives	A monthly archive of your site's Posts.	**Related Posts (YARPP)**	Related Posts and/or Sponsored Content
Audio	Displays an audio player.	**RSS**	Entries from any RSS or Atom feed.
Calendar	A calendar of your site's Posts.	**Search**	A search form for your site.
Categories	A list or dropdown of categories.	**Tag Cloud**	A cloud of your most used tags.
Custom HTML	Arbitrary HTML code.	**Text**	Arbitrary text.
Gallery	Displays an image gallery.	**Video**	Displays a video from the media library or from YouTube, Vimeo, or another provider.
Image	Displays an image.		
Meta	Login, RSS, & WordPress.org links.		
Navigation Menu	Add a navigation menu to your sidebar.		
Pages	A list of your site's Pages.		
Recent Comments	Your site's most recent comments.		
Recent Posts	Your site's most recent Posts.		

Most of those were pre-installed with WordPress, but can you spot one that was added by a plugin we installed earlier in the book?

Hopefully, you can see the potential of widgets.

As you've just seen, you are not limited to the widgets that come pre-installed with WordPress. Many plugins or services provide their own widgets that you can add to your website as you build it. For example, the YARPP widget will add a list of related posts to any widgetized area, in case you don't want them displayed after the post.

Basic HTML

When adding a text widget, one thing that will come in handy is some simple HTML code. For example, if you want to add some text with a link to another page, you'd just look up the HTML below for creating a hyperlink and insert it into your text widget accordingly.

A hyperlink

<a href="URL">LINK TEXT</a>

Just replace URL with the web address of the page you want to link to, and LINK TEXT with the word or phrase you want to be linked.

Example:

If you are interested, you can read my review of the <a href="http://blenderreview.com/waring">waring blender</a> for more details.

If I entered that into a sidebar text widget, it would look like this on my site:

EXAMPLE LINK

If you are interested, you can read my review of the waring blender for more details.

I added a title to the text widget (Example link). You can see the phrase "Waring blender" is a link to the URL I specified in the HTML.

An image

To insert an image, here is the HTML:

<img src="URL" width="XX" height="YY" />

Replace URL with the URL of the image (upload it via the media library and grab the URL there), XX is the width in pixels and YY is the height in pixels. If your image is the correct size (which it should be to keep image load times to a minimum), then you can leave out the height and width parameters and the code just becomes:

<img src="URL" />

For example, using an image from my media library, I grabbed the URL for the image and inserted it into a text widget. This is what it looks like:

IMAGE INSERTED

That's a 32-year-old me!

A numbered list

The HTML for a numbered list is a little more complicated.

```
<ol>
  <li>item one</li>
  <li>item two</li>
  <li>item three</li>
</ol>
```

You simply replace item one, item two, item three and so on with whatever you want displayed. You can add as many items as you need. Just repeat the <li>item</li> code once for each item you want to add.

For example, here is some code which shows a numbered list of my top three tablet recommendations.

```
<ol>
  <li>Asus 301</li>
  <li>Asus 201</li>
  <li>Apple iPad</li>
</ol>
```

.. and this is what it looks like in a sidebar text widget.

AN EXAMPLE LIST

1. Asus 301
2. Asus 201
3. Apple iPad

NOTE: The text you add for an item CAN be a hyperlink. Just construct it from the HTML I showed you above.

A bullet list

A bulleted list is almost the same code as the numbered list with one modification.

Instead of the code opening with <ol> and closing with </ol>, a bullet list opens with <ul> and closes with </ul>. The "ol" stands for ordered list (ordered by number), whereas the "ul" stands for unordered list.

<ul>

  <li>**item one**</li>

  <li>**item two**</li>

  <li>**item three**</li>

</ul>

Here is my widget now:

A BULLET LIST

- item one
- item two
- item three

That should give you enough HTML to get you started with text widgets.

There is one other widget that I do want to discuss in a little more detail. It goes hand-in-hand with one of the features we haven't looked at yet – custom navigation menus. The widget itself is used to display a custom menu in a widgetized area. We, therefore, need to create a menu, so that's what we'll be doing in the next chapter.

Tasks to complete

1. Go and explore the widgets area. Add some widgets to your site and then view the site in your browser to see what they do and how they format the information.

2. Add in a text widget and experiment with the HTML code I gave you in this chapter. Try adding a text widget to the top of the sidebar with a photograph of yourself and a brief bio.

Navigation menus

To add or edit a navigation menu in WordPress (called **Custom menus** in WordPress 4.8 and earlier), go to **Menus** inside the **Appearance** menu.

Let's design a menu for our website. In it, we'll add links to the legal pages we created – Contact, Privacy Policy, and Terms.

Add a name in the **Menu Name** box, and click the **Create Menu** button:

I've called my menu "Legal Menu" to reflect its purpose. This makes things easier when you have multiple menus and you are trying to decide which one is which.

On the left of the screen, you'll have a section that lists all Pages, Posts, Categories etc. Pull down the **Screen Options** and check Tags as well.

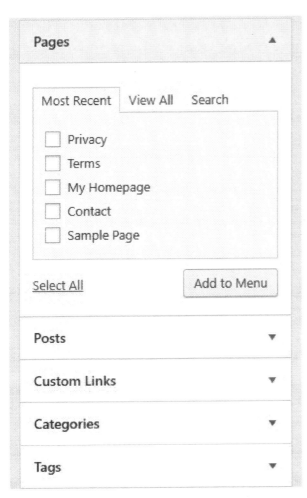

You can now add any post, page, category page or tag page to the menu.

Currently, the Pages section is expanded. You can see three tabs at the top: **Most Recent**, **View All** and **Search**. These will help you find a specific page, so you can insert it into the menu.

To expand a different section, simply click on the section. E.g. Posts:

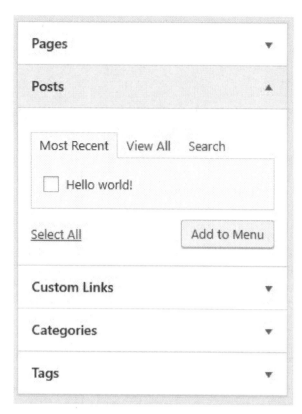

Pages collapse, and Posts open.

Since we want to add legal pages, click on the Pages section to expand it. We want the privacy policy, terms, and contact. If you can see them all on the **Most Recent** screen, check the box next to each one. If you don't see them all listed in most recent, click on view all, and you will find them there.

With all three checked, click the **Add to Menu** button:

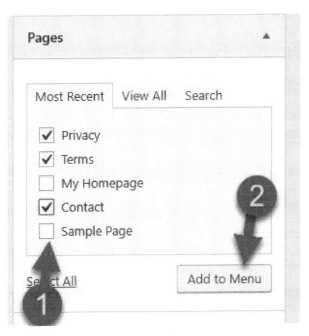

You will see all three added to the menu on the right-hand side of the screen:

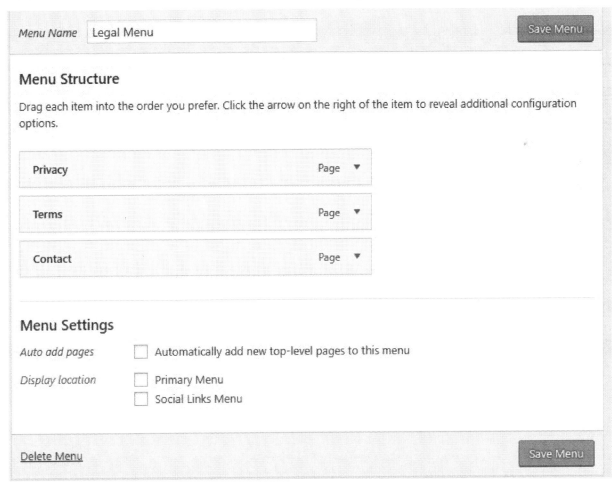

If you move your mouse over one of the items in the menu, the cursor changes:

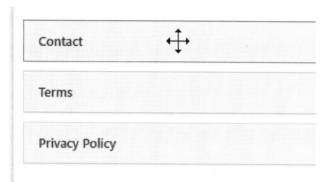

This cursor indicates that the item can be dragged and dropped. Click and drag it up or down to re-order the items in the menu. I want Terms at the top, then privacy, and contact at the bottom.

Under these three menu items are two other options:

Menu Settings

Auto add pages	☐ Automatically add new top-level pages to this menu
Theme locations	☐ Primary Menu
	☐ Social Links Menu

The **Auto Add Pages** option will automatically add new pages you create on the site to this menu. That typically isn't something we want, so leave it unchecked.

The second option defines the location of the menu within the theme. The Twenty Sixteen theme has two locations assigned to menus. One is the primary menu, and the other is the social links menu.

The social links menu is a special menu that should be used for your social media links (Facebook, Twitter, etc.), so we'll ignore that one. The Primary menu is across the top of the site, under the header. Check **Primary Menu** and then **Save Menu**. Now go and check out your website.

Harlun Limited

Company Website

Terms   Privacy   Contact

You can see the menu has been added to the top right. The Twenty Sixteen theme is responsive, so if you resize your browser window and make it smaller, the menu will collapse to a "Menu" button, and clicking the button will open the menu:

Harlun Limited

Company Website

Terms

Privacy

Contact

Have a play around with that. Add a menu, then resize your web browser window until the menu disappears into the menu button. Increase the size of your browser again to see the menu items re-appear.

Menu Hierarchy

It is possible to create hierarchical drop-down menus. In other words, each item in the menu can have a parent or child type relationship.

Using my menu above to illustrate, if I drag the privacy policy a little to the right, it becomes indented under the first one. Repeating this for the contact link result in this:

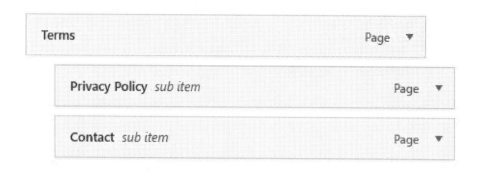

Save the menu and then visit your site again.

The menu will now just show the "parent" item, in this case, **Terms:**

Terms ⌄

Moving your mouseover Terms will open the menu:

This technique can be used to tidy up big menus with lots of items, but it does not make sense to do so in the above example. It's easy enough to fix though, just un-indent those items.

On the **Menus** screen, you'll probably have noticed two tabs at the top – **Edit Menus** and **Manage Locations**. The Edit Menus screen is the one we have been working in to create this menu. The Manage Locations screen is there to make it easier to manage multiple menus and place them in the predefined locations within the theme. Since Twenty Sixteen has two menu locations, you can see them both listed here, and you can choose which menu to insert into each, by selecting from the drop-down box:

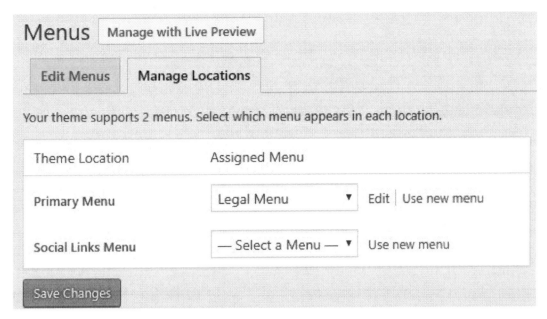

OK, switch back to the **Edit Menus** tab.

One other type of link that can be added to a menu is a custom link. You can see it listed there on the left. This allows you to link to any URL you like, and add that link to the menu.

To create a custom link, add the URL of the page you want to link to and the link text you want to appear, then click **Add to Menu.**

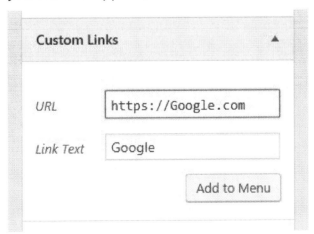

The link will be added to the menu.

Menu Structure

Drag each item into the order you prefer. Click the arrow on the right of the item to r
additional configuration options.

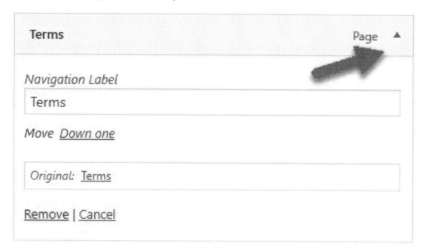

Custom links are labeled as such. Posts will be labeled as post, and pages are obviously labeled as page.

You may have noticed that each link in the menu has a little arrow on the far right. Click it to expand the options for that link:

At the bottom, you can **Remove** a menu item.

The default link settings only provide the options shown above, as some are hidden. Open the **Screen Options** and check the options for **Link Target** and **Link Relationship (XFN).**

You will now see two new items in the options:

The **Link target** creates the checkbox so you can choose to have menu links open in a new tab.

The **Link Relationship** allows you to add nofollow tags to your links. If you don't know what these are, don't worry. Simply put, the nofollow tag tells a search engine that a page you are linking to is not important. I often use these on links to my legal pages, like this:

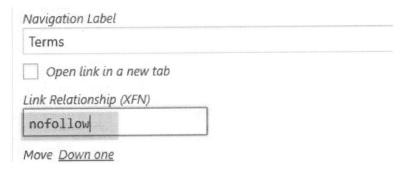

Edit an existing Menu

There will be times when you want to edit an existing menu. This is straightforward enough. Go to **Menus** in the **Appearance** menu.

If you only have one menu, that is the one you will see. If you have more than one menu created, use the drop-down box to choose the menu you want to edit:

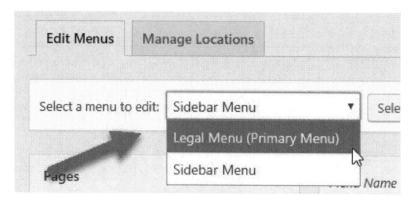

Click the **Select** button to switch to that menu and edit.

Navigation Menu Widgets

Any menu you create can be added to a sidebar (or any widgetized area) using the navigation menu widget.

First, I need to **Create a new menu**:

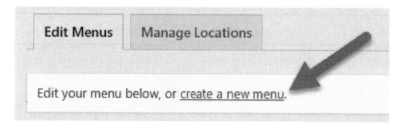

We create it the same way. Give your menu a meaningful name (I am calling mine **Sidebar Menu**) and click the **Create Menu** button.

I'll just add a couple of posts to the menu using the posts selector and then save my new menu.

OK, head back to **Widgets** in the **Appearance** menu.

When you get there, drag a **Navigation Menu** widget into the **Sidebar** area:

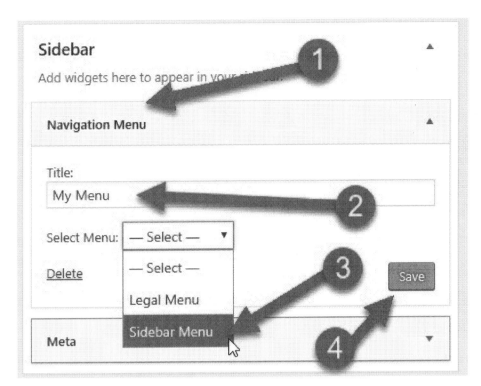

Add a title and select the menu from the drop-down box.

Save the widget, then check out the sidebar on your homepage. Here is mine:

MY MENU

- WordPress tutorial
- My Homepage

META

- Site Admin
- Log out
- Entries RSS
- Comments RSS
- WordPress.org

You can create navigation menus for all kinds of things. These may be top review pages or important tag pages. The point is this; custom menus give you the flexibility you need as you design and develop your website.

Tasks to complete

1. Go and experiment with Navigation Menus.
2. Create a menu with a "Home" link (custom link to homepage URL) and links to the "legal" pages on your site.
3. Add the menu to a widgetized area of your site.

Viewing your site while logged in

Something special happens when you are visiting your website while logged into the Dashboard.

Earlier, when we were looking at the User Profile, we made sure an option was checked - **Show Toolbar when viewing site.** Let's have a look what happens with that option enabled.

Log in to your dashboard and then open your website in another tab of your web browser.

What you'll see is a very useful "ribbon" across the top of your website:

This ribbon gives you access to some important WordPress features. For example, if you want to edit a page or post on your website, you can visit your website, find the post, then click on the edit post link in the ribbon bar (you can see it in the screenshot above). That will open the post in the WordPress Dashboard ready for editing.

The ribbon is very useful as you browse your site. If you find errors, just click the **Edit Post** link, fix the issue(s), and then click the **Update** button.

Some items in the menu have drop-down options.

Mouseover your site name on the left, and you'll have links to:

These links will take you directly to those areas of the Dashboard.

There is also a quick way to add new content to your site. Mouseover the **New** item to quickly add a new post, page, media item or user:

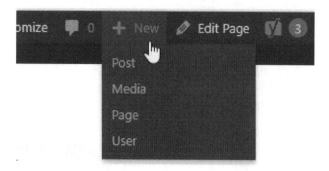

If you installed the Yoast SEO plugin, that adds a drop-down menu to the toolbar too, offering quick SEO links. I'll leave you to explore those.

Finally, on the right, if you mouseover your name, you'll get this menu:

These options are self-explanatory.

The ribbon has a couple of useful indicators too. If you have any updates that need installing, the update indicator will tell you:

If you mouse over this, it will tell you what needs updating. In my case, it's a plugin. Clicking the update indicator will take you to the **Update** section of the Dashboard.

There is also a speech bubble that represents comments awaiting moderation. If there are comments waiting, the speech bubble will tell you how many. In my case, I don't have any comments awaiting moderation:

Clicking the speech bubble will open the Dashboard on the moderation screen.

Tasks to complete

1. Login to your site.
2. Open the site in a new tab in your browser.
3. Mouseover, then click every option in the ribbon bar at the top. See what these links do and where they take you when you click them.

WordPress security

WordPress has often been criticized for being too easy to hack. There have been a lot of cases where people have lost their WordPress site after a hacker gained access to it and wreaked havoc. Several years ago, one of my sites got hacked so badly that I just deleted the whole thing and let the domain expire. At that time, I didn't have a reliable backup system in place.

We set up a plugin earlier called UpdraftPlus. That is creating backups for us, and it is a great start.

Another layer of protection is to **always upgrade WordPress** (and plugins) as soon as there is a new update available.

The WordPress team fix security leaks as soon as they are found. Therefore, if your Dashboard says there is a WordPress upgrade, install it as soon as possible to make sure your copy has all the bug fixes and/or security patches.

Finally, the All-in-One Security plugin we mentioned earlier is something I install on all my own sites. Do watch this video tutorial for a basic installation and setup of that plugin:

http://ezseonews.com/WordPresstutorials/all-in-one-wp-security-firewall/

For those that want more guidance on security, I have a full video course on the topic of WordPress Security and how to make sure your site is virtually hack-proof. If you want more details on that, please visit:

http://ezseonews.com/udemy

That page lists all my courses(with substantial discounts), so just look for the WordPress Security course if that is the one that interests you.

Tasks to complete

1. Make sure UpdraftPlus is making regular backups of your site and preferably storing them in the cloud, e.g. on Dropbox.
2. Always keep WordPress (and plugins) up to date.
3. Watch the free All in One Security Firewall video from the link above and consider setting it up to secure your website.

Monitoring website traffic

Every Webmaster wants to know how many visitors their site is getting and how those people are finding their pages (search engines, social media channels, etc.).

Fortunately, there are good (and free) solutions to give you this information.

The tool I use on my own sites is called **Google Analytics**, but it is complex and perhaps overkill for someone just starting out. I'd, therefore, recommend you check out a free service like "Get Clicky":

http://clicky.com/

I won't go into details on setting this up, but it is straightforward. You'll need to sign up for a free account and then install tracking on your website. This plugin can help with that:

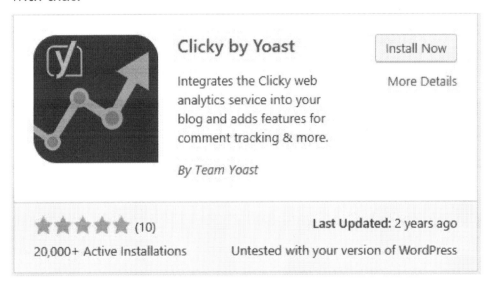

Once integrated into your site, Clicky will monitor your visitors. You'll get information about where they come from and what they do on your site.

As your site grows, I'd highly recommend you investigate Google Analytics and make the switch. It's the best free tool out there and gives a wealth of information about your visitors.

Tasks to complete

1. Install web analytics on your site. An easy option for beginners is to use the free services over at **Get Clicky**.

2. Install the "Clicky by Yoast" plugin and configure it as per the installation instructions on the plugin site.

3. Log in to your Get Clicky account and explore the reports and options. Use their help if needed.

4. When you have time, look into Google Analytics.

Appendix I - Moving a site from WordPress.com to WordPress.org

So, you've outgrown WordPress.com and want to move your content to a hosted WordPress.org website?

Switching to WordPress.org will remove limitations and give you a lot of new features and freedom. Fortunately making the switch is not too difficult. I should warn you though that not everything is moved across. Your content and images will be, as will categories and tags. That means the important stuff. You will need to change themes, add plugins, and generally set up, but your content will be safe.

Before you start the move, you need to have web hosting and a domain name. We covered hosting and registrars earlier in this book, so go back and make sure you have the domain and hosting set up.

Step 1 - Export your Data from WordPress.com

Log in to your WordPress.com website and click on the **Settings** menu in the left sidebar.

Scroll down the settings page until you find **Export** in the **Site Tools**.

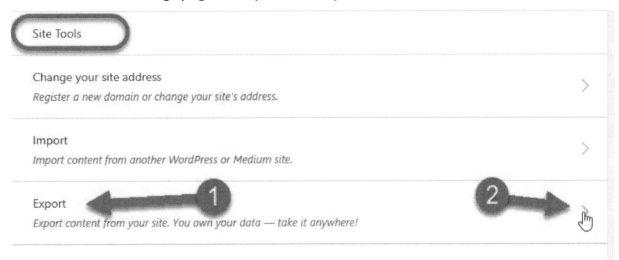

Click on the Export link.

The screen loads with an **Export All** button, but also a down arrow that opens a panel with more options:

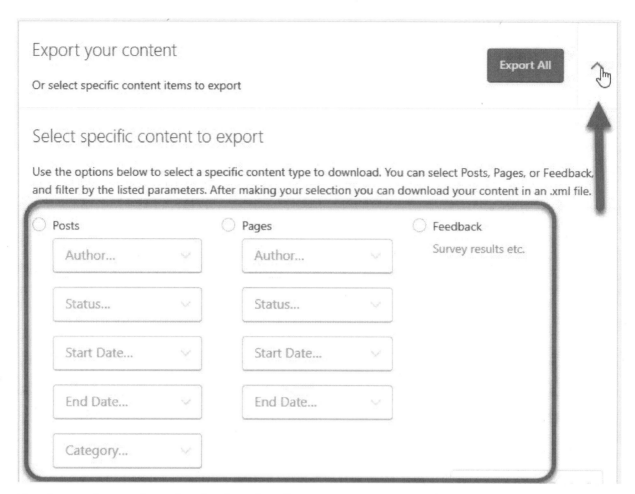

You have the option of only downloading posts or pages, plus you can control which posts or pages by specifying author, status, category, etc.

Once you have made your selection, click either the **Export Selected Content** or the **Export All** button if you want everything.

You will get a message saying the export was successful and a link was sent to your email address. However, you can also click the **Download** link to get the exported data:

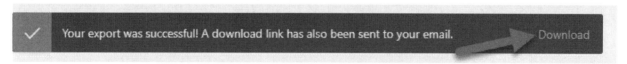

Step 2 – Import the Data into WordPress.org website

You've got your domain setup and WordPress installed (from WordPress.org). Log in to the dashboard of your domain.

From the **Tools** menu in the left sidebar, select **Import**.

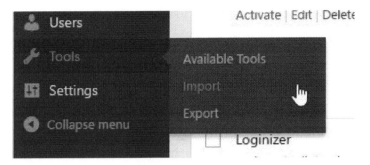

At the bottom of the screen, you'll see an option to import from WordPress. This is the option we will use, but first, we need to install a plugin by clicking the **Install Now** link:

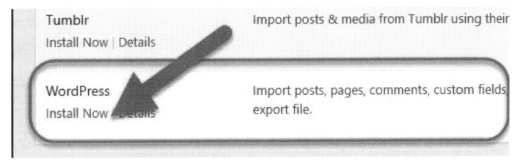

Once installed, that **Install Now** link changes to **Run Importer**. Click the Run Importer link. You will be asked to choose a file to import.

The file you downloaded was a zip file. That is a compressed file that you need to unzip first. There are various free tools available that can do this for you, so search Google for a free zip tool if you need one.

Once unzipped, your file will have an XML extension. This is the file we need to import. Click the **Choose file** button and select the unzipped XML file.

Once you've selected the file, click the **Upload File and Import** button.

The next screen will give you the option of supplying an author name for the content.

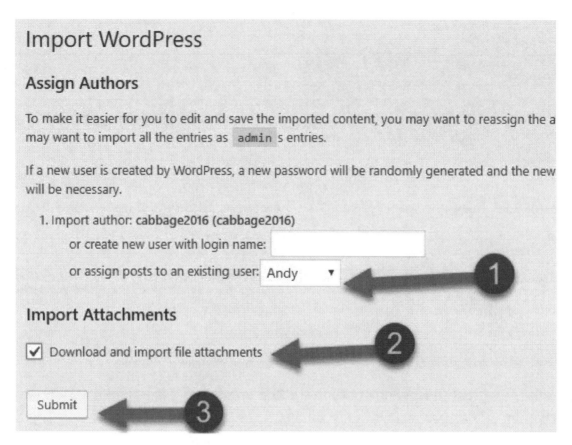

Import WordPress

Assign Authors

To make it easier for you to edit and save the imported content, you may want to reassign the a may want to import all the entries as `admin` s entries.

If a new user is created by WordPress, a new password will be randomly generated and the new will be necessary.

   1. Import author: **cabbage2016 (cabbage2016)**

      or create new user with login name:

      or assign posts to an existing user: Andy ▼   1

Import Attachments

☑ Download and import file attachments   2

Submit   3

Select the author of the content from the drop-down box, or type in a new user to assign the content to.

Check the box to **Download and import file attachments**.

Now click the **Submit** button.

You should get a message saying:

Import WordPress

All done. Have fun!

Remember to update the passwords and roles of imported users.

If you go to your site, you should see that the content is now incorporated into your site. To show this, I've added a category widget to the **Content Bottom 1** area:

My Homepage

Homepage content here

Edit

CATEGORIES

- Christmas Crafts
- Christmas Decorations
- Christmas Ideas
- Wordpress tutorial

You should find all the posts and pages have been imported into your site.

With all the content across on your hosted domain, you can now choose themes and plugins, and set the site up to look as you want. It should not take you too long to get the site looking the same, or better than before.

Step 3 – Redirect the WordPress.com site to your new domain

Once the content has been moved across, you will have two sites showing identical content. The same articles will be on your WordPress.com site and your hosted domain.

If your WordPress.com site does not have valuable links pointing to it and does not get any real search engine traffic, you can set the site to **Private**.

To do that, log in to your WordPress.com website and click on the **settings** menu. Scroll down to the **Privacy** section and choose **Private**:

Click the **Save Settings** button.

Your site will now only be visible to you, and search engines should start deindexing the content on that site.

If your WordPress.com site gets a lot of traffic from the search engines, or has valuable links pointing at it, you should redirect the old site to the new.

The problem is that you do not have access to the .htaccess file on WordPress.com to set up the redirects. The solution is to use a service provided by WordPress.com.

Login to your WordPress.com website and click on the **Settings** menu in the left sidebar.

On the setting screen, you will see a section called **Site Address**.

Click on the link to **redirect** this site.

You then have the option of signing up for the redirection service. At the time of writing, this service cost $13 per year.

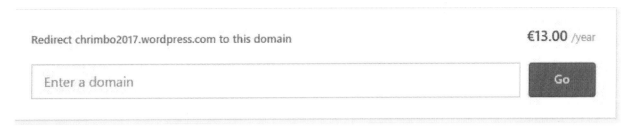

Redirect chrimbo2017.wordpress.com to this domain	€13.00 /year
Enter a domain	Go

Once you have the redirect in place, you can forget about your old WordPress.com website. At any time, you can cancel the redirection service, but if you do, make sure you also delete your WordPress.com website or you'll once again have your content duplicated on two websites.

Appendix II. Search Engine Optimization (SEO)

Search Engine Optimization has changed a lot in the last couple of years. It has always been one of the most important aspects of building a website because it helps you to rank better in Google, and consequently get more traffic, and make more sales from your pages.

Today, things are very different. If you overdo your optimization, Google is likely to penalize you and dump your site out of its search engine.

If you ask Google about the best way to optimize your site, it would probably tell you to avoid Search Engine Optimization altogether, focus on 'visitor experience', and not worry about search engines.

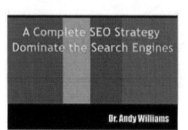

Despite sounding like a lost cause, you should still consider a number of "best practices" as you build your website. I will list the main things to consider here, but if you want a more in-depth discussion about SEO, I'd highly recommend my own book on the subject called **SEO 2017 & Beyond - Search Engine Optimization will never be the same again** (the 2018 version should be out soon).

It's available in Kindle Format and as a paperback on Amazon. I also have another book (and course) on WordPress-specific SEO. Check out the links later in this book to **My Other Webmaster Books**, and **My Video Courses**.

Main points for safe SEO

1. Always write content for the visitor, not the search engines.

2. Always create the highest quality content possible and make it unique. More than that, add something to your content that is not found on any other websites covering the same or similar topic. Use your personal voice, experiences, and thoughts.

3. Engage your visitor and allow them to open discussion with you through the built-in comment feature.

4. Never try to write content based on keyword phrases. Always write content on a topic. E.g. don't write an article on "best iPhone case", write an article on "Which iPhone Case offers the best protection for your phone?" See the difference?

5. As a measure of whether your content is good enough, ask yourself if you could imagine your article appearing in a glossy magazine? If you answer no, then it's not good enough to publish on your own website.

6. DO NOT hire people to build backlinks to your site. If you want to build some links, they need to be on high-quality web pages. You can find more specific advice in

my SEO book.

7. Add a social sharing plugin to your site so that people can quickly share your content on social channels like Facebook, Twitter, YouTube and Google Plus etc.

The best advice I can give you for present day SEO is to **read and digest Google's Webmaster Guidelines**. They are there to help us create sites that will rank well in their Search Engine Results Pages, aka SERPs. You can read those guidelines here:

http://ezseonews.com/wmg

Tasks to complete

1. Read Google's Webmaster Guidelines repeatedly until you know them off by heart. They really are very important and will benefit you in the long run; providing you adhere to their suggestions of course

Where to go from here?

We've covered a lot of ground in this book. You should now be confident finding your way around the WordPress Dashboard.

You have installed WordPress, installed the essential plugins, and configured everything so that your site is now ready for content.

So, what's the next step?

Create impressive content!

Everything we have done in this book has been to achieve one main goal. Get your site set up & ready to accept your content. You can now concentrate on publishing content while WordPress takes care of the rest.

Here is your plan going forward.

1. Create a post.
2. Publish it.
3. Rinse and repeat steps 1 and 2.

If you want a "static" homepage rather than one showing your recent posts, create a page with the content you want to be displayed there. Then set up the reading settings so that this page is shown permanently on your site's homepage. You can then go back to the 3-step process outlined above

Create a post, publish & repeat.

Good luck!

Andy Williams

Useful resources

There are a few places that I would recommend you visit for more information.

My other Webmaster books

All my books are available as Kindle books and paperbacks. You can view them all here:

http://amazon.com/author/drandrewwilliams

I'll leave you to explore those if you are interested. You'll find books on various aspects of being a webmaster, such as creating high-quality content, SEO, CSS etc.

My Video Courses

I have a growing number of video courses hosted on Udemy. You can view a complete list of these at my site:

http://ezseonews.com/udemy

There are courses on the same kinds of topics that my books cover, so SEO, Content Creation, WordPress, Website Analytics, etc.

Google Webmaster Guidelines

http://ezseonews.com/wmg – this is the webmaster's bible of what is acceptable and what is not in the eyes of the world's biggest search engine.

Google Analytics

http://www.google.com/analytics/ – the best free analytics program out there. When you have some free time to learn how to use Google Analytics, I recommend you upgrade from Get Clicky.

Please leave a review/thought on Amazon

If you enjoyed this book, or even if you didn't, I'd love to hear your comments about it. You can leave your thoughts on the Amazon website.

Index

Made in the USA
Middletown, DE
01 September 2018

The Christmas Tooth Fairy

By

MURLIE COLOSKY HANSON

Murlie C. Hanson

Illustrated by LAUREN C. OLIVEIRA

First Edition

Dedicated to Krista and Jenna who were my

inspiration and first editors.

Library of Congress Control Number: 2010908164
ISBN-13: 978-0-615-37678-3

O.M.O. Publications
P.O. Box 1454
Monterey, CA 93942

Writer: Murlie C. Hanson
Illustrator: Lauren C. Oliveira

www.TheChristmasToothFairy.com
www.OMOpublications.com

Printed in the United States of America

Bang Printing, 3323 Oak Street, Brainerd, MN 56401
#303145   7/2010

This book belongs to

The Christmas Tooth Fairy

Written by Murlie C. Hanson

Illustrated by Lauren C. Oliveira

"Hello, boys and girls. We are reporting live from our studio at K-ID TV, with our special guest, the Tooth Fairy.

"Welcome, Tooth Fairy. Our audience knows that your job is collecting baby teeth, and everyone is interested in knowing more about how you do that. Let's begin by having you tell us what a typical day is like for you."

4

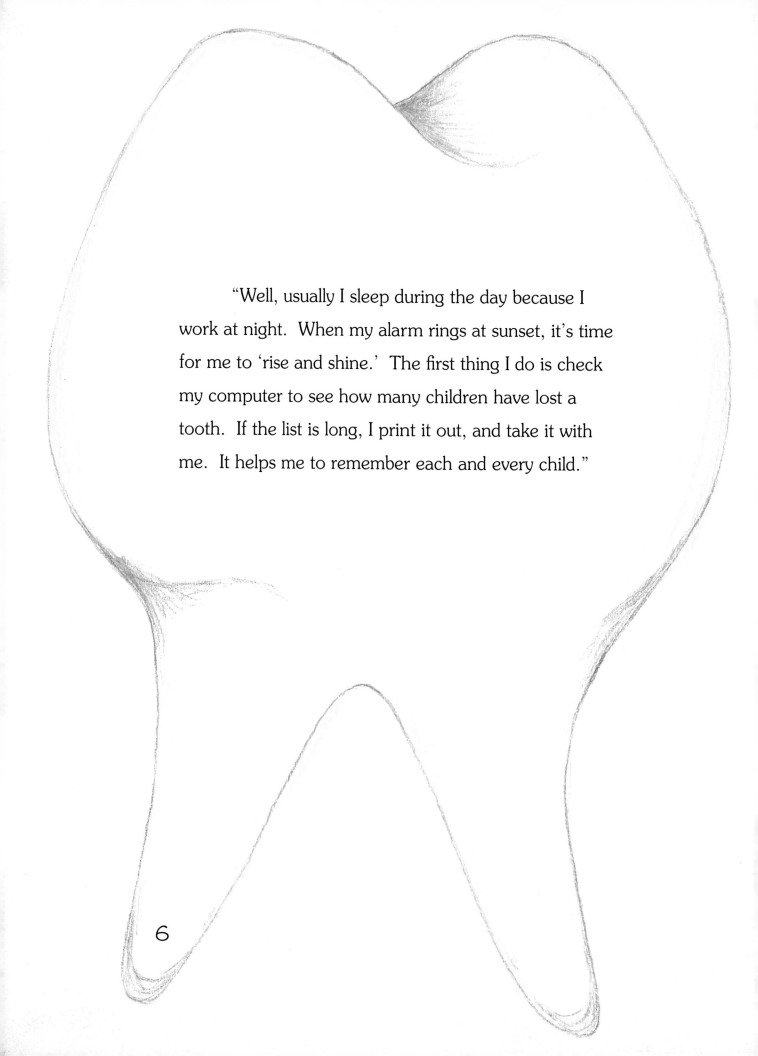

"Well, usually I sleep during the day because I work at night. When my alarm rings at sunset, it's time for me to 'rise and shine.' The first thing I do is check my computer to see how many children have lost a tooth. If the list is long, I print it out, and take it with me. It helps me to remember each and every child."

6

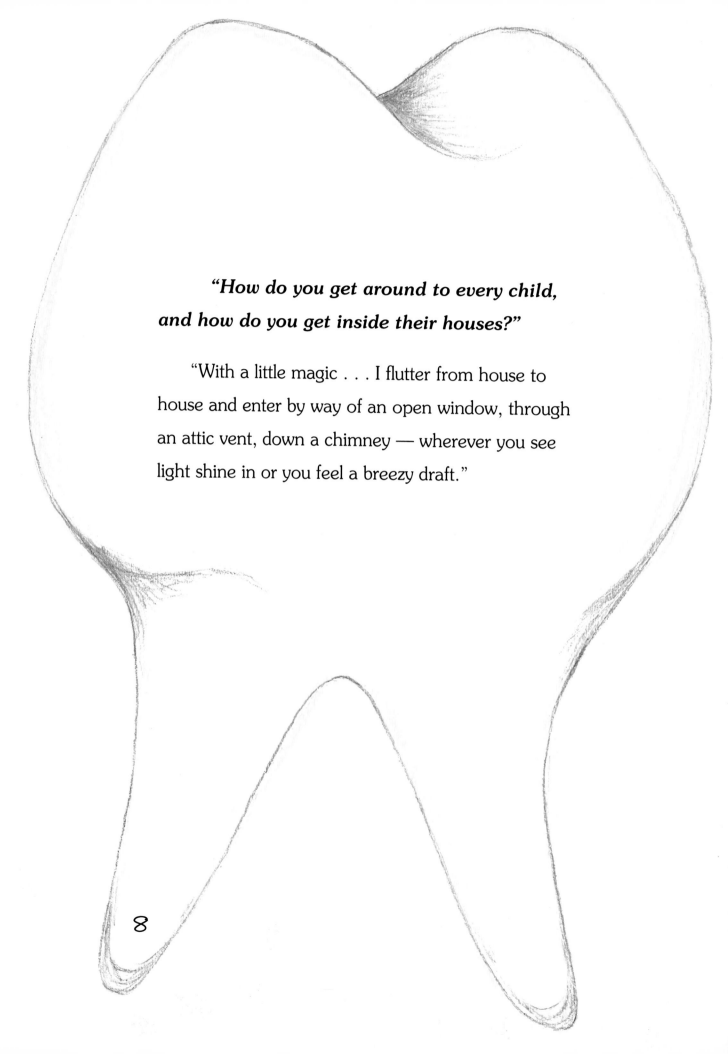

"How do you get around to every child, and how do you get inside their houses?"

"With a little magic . . . I flutter from house to house and enter by way of an open window, through an attic vent, down a chimney — wherever you see light shine in or you feel a breezy draft."

8

"As I look at you, I can see that your tiny size allows you to get into the bedrooms and reach under the pillows without waking the children, but how do you carry all of the money that you give to them? It must be very heavy."

"It is heavy, and I'm too small to carry it, so I turn the money into dust — gold dust — by saying these magic words:

**"Up and around, and down you go,
Into the bag as light as snow."**

10

Up and around,
and down you go,
Into the bag as
light as snow.

"But children find money, not gold dust, under their pillows."

"Yes, most of the time that's true, but boys and girls do not always leave the tooth under a pillow, so I sprinkle gold dust wherever I find a tooth. Then I gently tap my magic wand and whisper 10 simple words:

Dust of magic, colored honey,
Change your form, into money.

"And in a flash, the gold dust changes into money. Sometimes a child gets more money, sometimes less, only because there is no time to weigh and measure the dust."

12

Dust of magic,
colored honey,
Change your form,
into money.

"Oh, now I see why you need magic. So, Tooth Fairy, what do you like best about your job?"

"Without a doubt, the best part is receiving letters from children. I remember one letter from a little boy who explained why I didn't find his tooth under his pillow — he had swallowed it! And then there was the goodbye letter a little girl wrote after she lost her last baby tooth — number 20. I do love finding letters from children, but usually I find just a tooth."

14

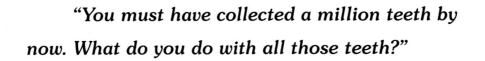

"You must have collected a million teeth by now. What do you do with all those teeth?"

"I use some of them—the best ones are teeth that were brushed often. I have teeth all over my house! I use them for furniture, for decorating, and even for jewelry. But most of the teeth I collect are turned into sparkles of stardust."

16

"Sparkles of stardust? How do you do that, Tooth Fairy?"

"By waving my magic wand over a tooth and singing these magic words:

Tooth so bright and colored white,
You shall be a star tonight.

"Then I toss the stardust into the night sky, and it becomes a twinkling star for all to wish upon. Sometimes, I save the sparkles from a lot of teeth and scatter them all at once, so that all can see, along with me, the night light up with shooting stars."

18

Tooth so bright
nd colored white,
You shall be a
star tonight.

"Is that what you do every night, even on holidays?"

"It was, until Christmastime a few years ago."

"What happened then?"

"It all started a few days before Christmas. You can imagine how busy December can be collecting all the extra teeth lost on sticky candy canes. Well, one night I was exhausted, and I dozed off before setting my alarm clock. The next thing I knew, I overslept. I jumped out of bed and immediately went to work collecting teeth. To make up lost time, I saved the notes children left under their pillows, to be read later, and I didn't search for hidden teeth lost in wrinkled sheets. My goal was to see each child. And I might have made it, if only I had skipped just one house."

20

"What house was that?"

"The one where the child had a very messy room. There were boxes stacked over the air vents, toys jammed against the windowsill, and clothes piled on the floor. That bedroom looked like it had been hit by a tornado. There was only one way for me to get in — through the key hole.

22

"As I tried to go under the pillow to get the
tooth, the child rolled over, and a stuffed bear toppled
toward me. I remember stumbling and fluttering
quickly to catch my balance, and all of a sudden my
delicate wing tore on the edge of an open drawer. I
couldn't fly with only one wing, so I couldn't collect
all of the teeth on my list. I knew children everywhere
would be so disappointed."

24

"How did you get home with a torn wing?"

"It took me a while to figure out a way. There was glue hidden in the clutter, and I almost missed it because tears welled in my eyes and made it difficult to see. But I used the glue, and it held my wing together just long enough to fly home.

26

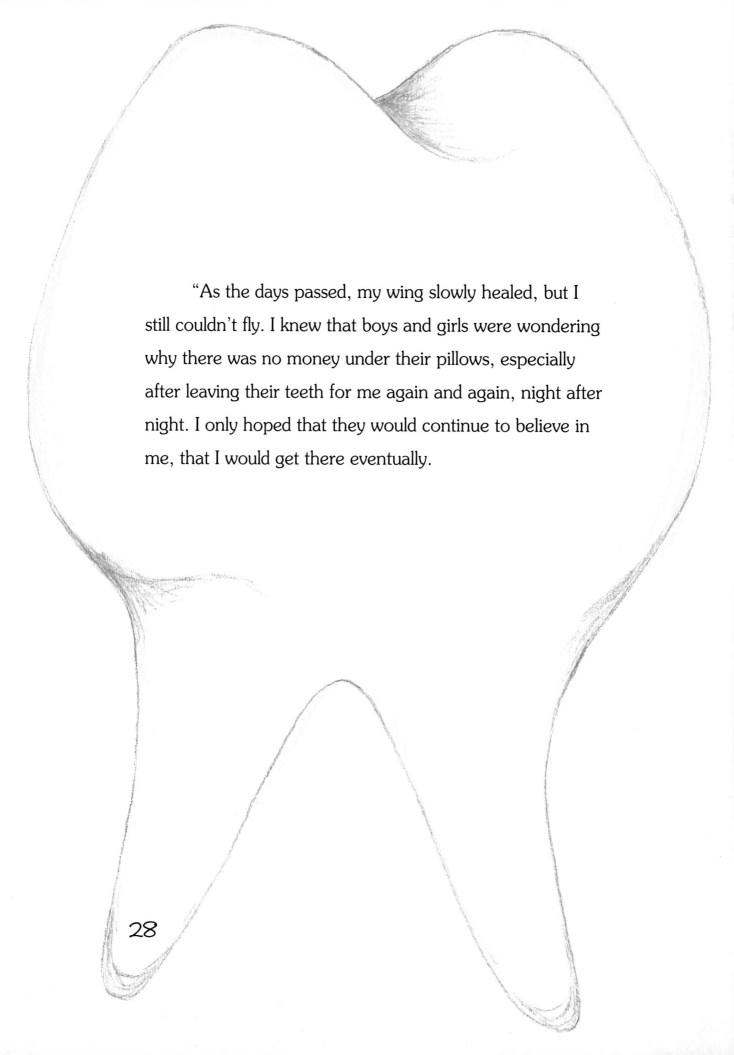

"As the days passed, my wing slowly healed, but I still couldn't fly. I knew that boys and girls were wondering why there was no money under their pillows, especially after leaving their teeth for me again and again, night after night. I only hoped that they would continue to believe in me, that I would get there eventually.

28

"I tried to think of other ways to get around so I could get back to work. Then on Christmas Eve, an idea came to me. What about Santa Claus? He's magical. He enters houses without being seen. He doesn't need a magic wand to turn teeth into stardust because he is big and strong, and he can carry a huge bagful of teeth just as they are. He doesn't need magical gold dust either, because he has a sleigh that's sturdy enough for heavy money and reindeer capable of pulling the load. And best of all, children believe in him."

30

"So did you call Santa at the North Pole?"

"Yes, but first I thought about it carefully, knowing on one hand that Santa Claus has a lot to do on Christmas Eve. Then on the other hand, knowing that he would be stopping at every house. So, I finally decided to call him and explain what had happened to my wing. He was hesitant."

"'There is one problem,' he said. 'I only stop at houses where children have been good. There might not be enough time for me to visit everyone.'"

"'I understand,' I told him. 'And that works for me.'"

32

"Santa collected the teeth that Christmas Eve and stopped by my house before returning to the North Pole. I can still hear the sound of his voice.

"'Ho-Ho-Ho,' he chuckled hello. He told me that on every rooftop he checked my 'baby tooth list,' and double-checked his 'naughty or nice list.' Inside, where it was warm and cozy, he tasted the milk and cookies the children left for him as he read the notes the children left for me. Santa told me that he had never enjoyed himself more on Christmas Eve, and he wished that he could do this every year."

34

"Since then, has Santa Claus collected the baby teeth every Christmas Eve?"

"Yes, he has, because having a vacation every year sounded like a good idea to me, and remember, he did make a wish. So, I twirled about his jolly self, waved my magic wand, and recited these magic words:

"Santa, you have wished
To bring good cheer,
As a tooth fairy,
To kids each year.
I grant your wish,
And on Christmas Eve,
You get the teeth
From kids who believe."

36

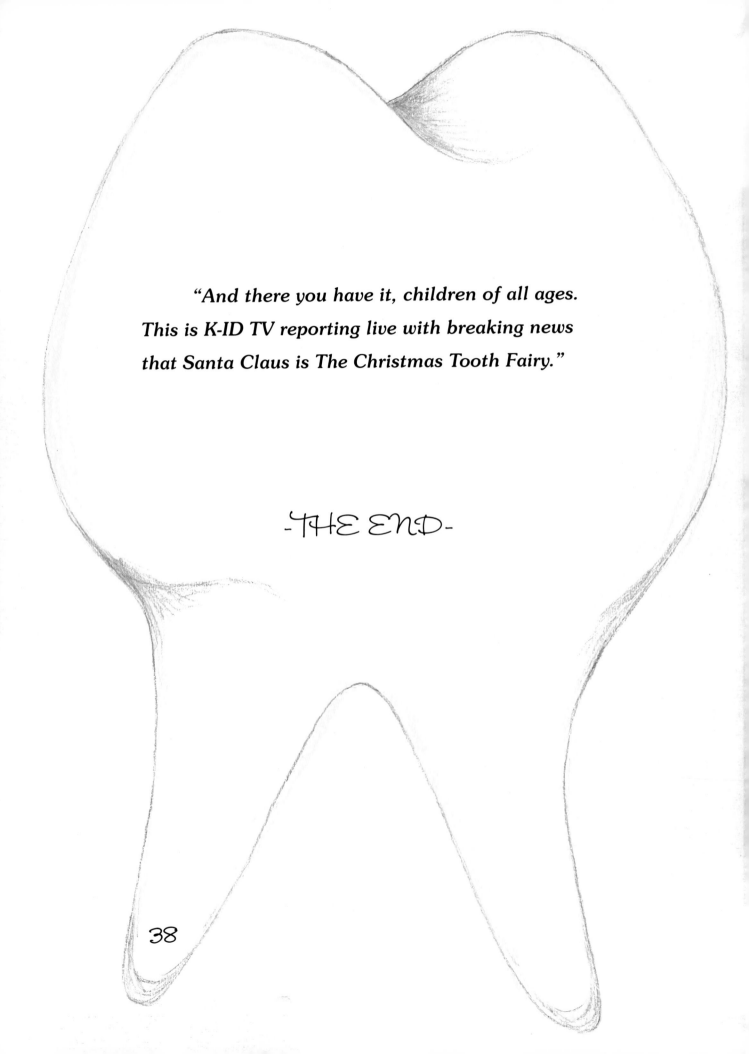

"And there you have it, children of all ages. This is K-ID TV reporting live with breaking news that Santa Claus is The Christmas Tooth Fairy."

-THE END-

38

"An innovative, delightful story, with creative answers to age-old questions about the tooth fairy. An enjoyable children's book for reading while enhancing the fanciful and mystical imagination."

Dr. William Barr, Super.of Schools (Ret.) Monterey Co. CA, and Faculty member, Graduate School of Education, U.C.Berkeley

"A magical story for children of all ages…."

Barbara C., Pebble Beach, CA

"A fun story with engaging illustrations. This book is also a useful tool for parents to teach their kids important life lessons about seeking solutions and considering consequences."

Terry F. General Manager, The Salinas Californian

"I love it. What a delightful 'O'Henry' ending! I never saw it coming. I can't wait to read it to my students… An amazing take on one of my favorite lessons, 'Where there's a will, there's a way.'"

Amelia H., Teacher, Fulton, MS.

"This is a great book! I love the story. I also like the chants. I remember all four of them. I am going to tell my friends all about them."

Francesca T., age 6

"Great read aloud that brings together two unexpected characters in a clever and unique way. The pictures are captivating and will pull children into this surprising story about teamwork and problem solving."

Valerie R., Kindergarten Teacher

"Murlie Hanson has created an imaginative children's story that artfully blends the contemporary with the classic. A twist on the traditional fairy tale, this bedtime story gives kids and adults alike the chance to believe in magic." -

Katie P., Freelance Writer

"This charming and utterly delightful story is a joy to read. Well-told and illustrated magically, …it is sure to capture your child's imagination in a most wonderful way!"

Debra C., Interior Designer - Carmel, CA